Holiness as a Liberal Art

Holiness as a Liberal Art

Edited by
Daniel Castelo

PICKWICK *Publications* · Eugene, Oregon

HOLINESS AS A LIBERAL ART

Copyright © 2012 Wipf and Stock Publishers. All rights reserved. Except for brief quotations in critical publications or reviews, no part of this book may be reproduced in any manner without prior written permission from the publisher. Write: Permissions, Wipf and Stock Publishers, 199 W. 8th Ave., Suite 3, Eugene, OR 97401.

The Scripture quotations contained herein (unless otherwise noted) are from the New Revised Standard Version Bible, copyright © 1989 by the Division of Christian Education of the National Council of the Churches of Christ in the U.S.A., and are used by permission. All rights reserved.

Pickwick Publications
An Imprint of Wipf and Stock Publishers
199 W. 8th Ave., Suite 3
Eugene, OR 97401
www.wipfandstock.com

ISBN 13: 978-1-60899-505-9

Cataloging-in-Publication data:

Holiness as a liberal art / edited by Daniel Castelo.

xii + 122 p. ; 23 cm. — Includes bibliographical references.

ISBN 13: 978-1-60899-505-9

1. Holiness. 2. Education, Humanistic—United States. I. Title.

BX8331.3 H64 2012

Manufactured in the U.S.A.

To our trusty and tireless theological librarian,

Steve Perisho

Contents

Contributors

Contributors to this volume are associated with Seattle Pacific University in the following ways:

Daniel Castelo, Ph.D.
Associate Professor of Theology

Robert R. Drovdahl, Ph.D.
Professor of Educational Ministry

Kelsie Gayle Job
Graduate Student in Biblical Studies

Jeffrey F. Keuss, Ph.D.
Professor of Christian Ministry, Theology, and Culture

Douglas M. Koskela, Ph.D.
Associate Professor of Theology

Michael D. Langford, Ph.D.
Assistant Professor of Theology

David R. Nienhuis, Ph.D.
Associate Professor of New Testament Studies

Priscilla Pope-Levison, Ph.D.
Professor of Theology and Assistant Director of Women's Studies

Frank Anthony Spina, Ph.D.
Professor of Old Testament and Biblical Theology

Mark P. Stone
Graduate Student in Theological Studies

Holiness as a Liberal Art

Douglas M. Strong, Ph.D.
Dean and Professor of the History of Christianity

Robert W. Wall, Th.D.
Paul T. Walls Professor of Scripture and Wesleyan Studies

Introduction

ONE OF THE MOST difficult topics to register among Christians today is the notion of holiness. When holiness is considered as a thematic to guide our lives, people often are skeptical. Frankly, the church, as the culture more broadly, is suspicious of putting anybody on a pedestal as "holy" because we are all human, and so we are all frail and fall short. Interestingly enough, *we are more sympathetic toward acknowledged fragility than to failed striving.* Such a scenario has a way of granting grace to ourselves as well, for if falling short is part of what it means to be human, then we do not have to be too hard on ourselves when we mess up; in fact, we can complacently give up before we even get started since we all know that everybody is weak and imperfect. Leading such a life throws in the towel before it even gets started; such is a defeatist attitude.

But do we always have to mess up in the same way over and over again? Is life one potential failure in all things spiritual? Aren't we called to be victors in this life? The Bible suggests that there are stages in the spiritual life; some are weak, and others are strong; in the faith, some are adults, others young, and finally some are children. Do we really believe that these levels exist?

And if they do, then shouldn't we be about striving and running this race, putting everything we have into it rather than sitting back in the stands because we know we can't make it? Isn't it true that if we don't try, we are doomed to fail, but if we do try, we become all the better in the process?

This small book has two purposes. One purpose is to initiate a conversation about holiness. Why holiness? Because the contributors to this volume adhere to a very important premise: To live a vibrant Christian life is to lead a life of holiness. As Christians, we are called to be saints. God commands us to be holy because God is holy, and without holiness, we will not see God. A holy life is not easy; it sounds too daunting. But the Christian life is something to grow into; we were not born into adults; neither are we simply mature Christians when we come to faith. The Christian life is sufficiently deep and complex that there is always more to see, live, and embody.

A second, and more important, purpose of this book is to invite its readers into the depths of the holy life; before settling on what is and is not possible, of what can and can't happen, why don't we just see where the road takes us? Can we operate from an imagination that does not assume ahead of time the possibilities of what it means to follow Jesus in this life? Can we keep the possibilities open? We hope this little volume helps in the fostering of just such an imagination, for if we are keen on following God wherever God leads, the road often cannot be anticipated in terms of its twists and turns, but its formative and final goal makes such a life meaningful; this is the life of perfection. We hope you come to recognize that the holy life is the only life worth living. Along with Gregory of Nyssa, we hope you come to see that in following this holy God in the path of holiness, infinity is the only limit.

1

Cultivating a Sanctified Way of Life

Introducing Holiness as a Liberal Art

Daniel Castelo

WHAT IS THE POINT of *Christian higher education?* It is no secret that attending a Christian college or university[1] is an expensive ordeal, especially when compared to a community college or state university, and so the question persists: What is the benefit of the Christian college experience? One suspects that both parents and students have their varied reasons for opting for this possibility, but I would argue that the point of Christian higher education is to make us better disciples of Christ, or to put it in more controversial terms, to help us grow in holiness. Several claims have to be unpacked and elaborated for this thesis to be sustained, but ultimately, the reason such places as Christian colleges and universities exist is so that we can grow in the calling that Christ has extended to us: to be his disciples and witnesses in a corrupt, broken, and hurting world.

---

1. When speaking of Christian institutions of higher learning, I will use both "college" and "university" interchangeably.

Education as a Moral Enterprise

First of all, it is important to realize that education is a moral enterprise. Many scholars and institutions fail to recognize this point because it is a serious and controversial claim; after all, if education is morally forming then its appeal, as it is negotiated in our context, will be limited since it is not properly "value-free" and so generalizable to a wider, diverse public; however, despite the claims otherwise, there is no such thing as a non-formative, and so value-free, education. All pedagogies assume something about human beings, including what they are and what they are meant to be.[2] In this regard, then, pedagogies are moral, not only in the way they operate (the descriptive factor) but also in what they see as worth inculcating and producing (the prescriptive element). "All education, whether acknowledged or not, is moral formation."[3]

In our society, we tend to emphasize results or the bottom-line, and this perspective promotes a certain moral framework, one that assumes that what is good is what is monetarily profitable. And so, educational institutions are often pressured (especially as costs rise) to make a utilitarian case for the "product" they offer. The reasoning goes, "You ought to have something to show for all that time and money, so what can you do, and how can you earn a living with it?" Although all institutions of higher learning should take inventory of their processes and activities, this "bottom-line" approach just described is more appropriate for professional or trade schools; these places emphasize the development and mastery of certain skills so that people can in turn profit from the tendering of specific services.

Liberal arts colleges and universities are not strictly trade or professional schools. Many people wish that they would be so,

---

2. A work that pushes this logic to its revealing conclusions, both in terms of the broader educational enterprise and Christian higher education particularly, is James K. A. Smith's *Desiring the Kingdom*.

3. Hauerwas, *The State of the University*, 46.

especially in hard economic times, and their failure to be these kinds of schools tends to place the liberal arts curriculum under fire. "After all," people ask, "what is the point of the liberal arts curriculum? Why did people develop and promote this kind of educational model to begin with since it doesn't 'do' anything?" A liberal arts education is a contested enterprise, one with a long history and a number of intellectual, political, and economic factors to consider. Space constraints do not allow for a sufficiently adequate survey, but some points will be raised.

"Liberal education" was conceived and promulgated in ancient, democratic Greece. The understanding was that an educated citizenry was required for the *polis* (the city-state) to flourish. Citizens needed to engage one another effectively, persuasively, and "freely,"[4] so a set curriculum came to be established, one that focused on the "liberal arts." In medieval times, these arts included both literary (the *trivium*: grammar, logic, rhetoric) and mathematical (the *quadrivium*: arithmetic, geometry, music, and astronomy) disciplines. Notice that these areas of study are called liberal *arts*; the assumption here is that these fields require a certain kind of apprenticeship and a sustained fostering of skill within the broader rubric of aesthetics. For the ancient world, these skills were a species of *techne*, a term that does not denote so much a "technique" as a skill that was cultivated and disciplined and had its register in one's mind and spirit more so than one's hands. For this reason, people often assume a liberal education coincides with the fostering of such skills as critical thinking, persuasive communication (both written and oral), analytical prowess, and imaginative energy. Take note that these skills are not trades or professions that are immediately "profitable," but they are nevertheless vitally important for human flourishing.

4. The "liberal" in "liberal education" or "liberal arts," then, should not be taken to refer to the "liberal vs. conservative" political landscape; rather, "liberal" in this context implies "free" thinking and reflection, "free" in terms of being genuinely expressed by the thinker and "free" to explore and cultivate what was assumed by many as an innate human desire, namely the desire to know (Aristotle, *Metaphysics*, I, 1) and to flourish.

Why? Trades and types of professional training often focus on mastering a certain tangible, commodifiable skill, but they rarely venture to ask such questions as, "What do we live for? How should we live? What is good, beautiful, and true?" In our society, perhaps we do not think these are important questions (given the relative infrequency with which we discuss them in the public realm), but if we are inclined to devalue these concerns, then the future of our *polis* is in dire straits. As some authors have remarked, our times are "the most technologically advanced in history, with more technically skilled people per square mile than could once have been imagined," and yet within this context "genocide is a term with which every grade school child must become familiar."[5] People have harnessed the sheer skill and competency to annihilate millions of people in a very short period of time. Sadly, it takes such promethean proportions to press the question: "Wow, we *can* do this now. But *should* we?" The "should" here implies a moral framework; the liberal arts help raise the question of discerning and cultivating what is good and in turn resisting and opposing what is evil.

The Academy and the Church

John Wesley, in setting out the "General Rules" for his societies, offered the following three: 1) doing no harm/avoiding evil, 2) doing good, and 3) attending to all the ordinances of God.[6] An education at a Christian liberal arts college can focus on and discern all three in a way that a secular university cannot; it also can do so in a way that a local church cannot.

The secular university as a public institution is deeply contested, largely due to the ambiguity and abstraction of its purposes and aims. With the oft-repeated denial of its moral qualities, the modern-day secular university has a difficult time accounting for

5. Flannery and Newstad, "The Classic Liberal Arts Tradition," 4.

6. See "The Nature, Design, and General Rules of the United Societies," 69–73.

its purpose and constituency.[7] Given this self-imposed ambiguity and "placelessness," the university within the public realm often resembles and promotes the wider aims of the culture in which it finds itself. This reality presents an irony: rather than being an institution of "free thinking" (which, presumably, would imply calling into question what currently takes place within the public realm), the university often simply reflects the aims and values of its broader orbit. This state of affairs is in tension with the ancient model of liberal education. In that model, the academy prepared an up-and-coming citizenry for service; in our current model, the society significantly determines what kind of citizenry it wants its universities to produce. Now, of course, the matter has always been a two-way street, but in our current situation, the traffic appears to lean significantly in one direction. Rather than being an agent of change, the modern university tends be an agent of conformity.[8]

7. The following questions are repeatedly pressed by Hauerwas because they are not easily answerable in the case of the modern-day university: "What is the university for? Whom does it serve?" (*The State of the University*, passim).

8. This observation raises the question of just how "critical" is the "critical thinking" that modern universities so often claim they seek to foster. This point is brought to light by Alasdair MacIntyre: The popular understanding is that "One's education is to be useful to one in reaching certain goals [that have been devised beforehand]." However, MacIntyre, in a turn of reasoning that is audacious and bold, remarks,

> Against this, I want to suggest that what education should be about is the transformation of students' conceptions of their goals. The desire, the needs, the goals that people bring to their education are in general going to be as corrupt as the culture that produced them. So they are going to have to be transformed as persons. Aristotle pointed out that what pleases and pains the virtuous person is very different from what pleases and pains the vicious person, and both again are different from what pleases the merely immature person. Morality thus is in a very important way educative of desire. And the desires that people bring to their education are ones which they are going to have to modify, or even abandon, if they are to acquire the intellectual and moral virtues. If we treat the students' desires as given,

5

As for the church, a number of pressures exist in modern society that works against its sheer survival. Suspicions both external and internal to the church make it a kind of fellowship that one is reluctant to identify with or sacrifice for.[9] Pastors find themselves in need of appealing to the masses and quickly applying the scriptures to people's everyday lives and struggles. Within this context of suspicion, contention, and pressure, the church oftentimes has curbed its teaching role in terms of allotted time, resources, or topics that are discussed. The lowest common denominator is often pursued, both biblically and theologically, so as to appeal to the most people.

Those institutions of higher learning that actively promote and negotiate a Christian identity can do a number of things that the above two locations cannot. On the one hand, Christian colleges have a clearer sense of purpose than the modern secular university. Whereas the latter seeks to promote its values and aims in "value-less" and "unbiased" ways, the Christian university transparently recognizes that its pedagogy is moral and that its mission is decisive for its existence.[10] In relation to the church,

the students' original goals as given, we are in effect abdicating from the task of educating them into the intellectual and moral virtues." ("Values and Distinctive Characteristics of Teaching and Learning in Church-Related Colleges," as quoted in Hauerwas, *The State of the University*, 128–29n14)

9. In my experience, many of my students operate with the understanding that one can be a Christian apart from the church; however, rarely do they have the ability (or felt need) to identify the location whence they can make this kind of judgment.

10. To state the matter in a different way: Non-partisanship is a form of partisanship; no neutral approach to knowledge exists; for this reason, Charles Scriven can remark, "Teaching and learning in the Christian setting, including the Christian college, should honor and reflect the church's narrative. . . . Christian colleges, without embarrassment and without apology, should be *partisan*" ("Schooling for the Tournament of Narratives," 274). In fact, this kind of admission and call makes Christian education more self-revealing than those places that employ covert strategies of hiding behind "value-neutral" pedagogies. Christian schools can be more honest because they are more up-front about their commitments. This general strategy of recognizing that

the Christian college can talk about truth, beauty, goodness, justice, and other matters in a sustained way, one that draws from the vast disciplinary fields of human knowledge all the while acknowledging that the triune God is the source and end of all that is. The conversations that can happen at a Christian university are deeper and broader than those that can happen at a local church, yet the aims of both contexts significantly overlap.

Christian institutions of higher learning are more than church-related institutions; they are in a pivotal way ecclesially-based institutions:[11] They serve the wider church (and by extension, the broader world) by facilitating contexts in which truth, beauty, and goodness are discussed and engaged in a sophisticated and extensive manner, all the while with the recognition that the service we ought to render is one in which we worship and love God with all our hearts, minds, souls, and strength.[12] The church and the Christian college offer two communities of formation and discourse in which we can learn and grow as faithful followers of Christ.

---

all traditions are contextual is a move heralded by Alasdair MacIntyre. For a chapter that works from such assumptions, see Ian S. Markham, "The Idea of a Christian University."

11. I draw this nomenclature from the book *Conflicting Allegiances* edited by Budde and Wright. Although the contributors to this volume believe that an "ecclesially-based" institution does not exist as they have defined it, I believe that Christian colleges with faith mission statements are called to be more than simply "church-related."

12. Smith is helpful here: "In short, the Christian college is a *form*ative institution that constitutes part of the teaching mission of the church" (*Desiring the Kingdom*, 34). Smith continues to state that this formative dimension is related not simply to our intellectual formation but even more pressingly and fundamentally with the formation of our desires. According to Smith, whose logic derives from Augustine, humans are primarily not so much knowers as lovers.

The Cultivation of Convictions

When students start to plumb truth, beauty, and goodness, strange things often happen. They start to realize they had gifts that they didn't know they had. More importantly, they start to develop passions for causes, peoples, and issues that they knew very little or nothing about prior to their college careers. Although it is always dangerous to generalize, I have seen this pattern occur many times during my tenure as a college professor.

A typical scenario may look like this: As a student engages topics in class, she comes to develop a curiosity to find out more about an issue that intrigued her in class discussion and lecture. She looks up the matter on the internet and maybe attends a brown-bag discussion on campus. Soon, her eyes are opened to how big of an issue this specific topic is, and she starts to feel compelled to do something. She may attend a screening of a recent movie on the subject and even inquire about a school-sponsored trip to a region of the world where this issue is prominent. She ends up going there over the summer in order to see first-hand how the issue plays out in that context. What occurs subsequently could be a change in major, a change in vocation, in short, a change that marks her entire life. The issue in question is not the important matter; it could take any number of forms (human trafficking, access to clean drinking water, and many, many others); what is most important is the sense of passion and commitment that is cultivated.

What is going on here? If these movements are taking place within an explicit context of worship, a place where one's life and how one lives that life are expressions of faithfulness, obedience, and love to a God who is the source and end of all, then one cannot help but suggest that the work of God's Spirit is at play at such moments in the formation of what can be termed "spiritual convictions." Convictions are those commitments that fundamentally alter us, that make us who we are because they claim us in a very deep way.[13] Without them, we would not be ourselves because we humans are what we love; we are what we are passionate about. And if we are passionate about God and God's work of healing and repair in the world, then that passion is going to come through in any number of correspondences that can begin to take shape at a Christian college or university. Such places provide certain conditions so that the Spirit can work in the lives of God's people for the purposes of readying them for their call unto the world. Medical missions, non-profit organizations, charity work, preaching, teaching, nursing, essentially the whole gamut of professional possibilities are conceived by Christian colleges as vocations, as callings by the holy triune God made unto God's people for the hallowing of God's name and the sanctification of the world.

Holiness and Discipleship

I have just used a number of terms that may sound strange at this point. Holiness, hallowing, and sanctification sound like odd and obtuse words. What does holiness or making holy (hallowing/sanctifying) have to do with Christian higher education? Are these words not antiquated and useless to begin with?

As the essays in this collection will repeatedly state, holiness is a word that has a number of connotations within Christian discourse, and usually, these are unfortunately negative. For many Christians, the term "holy" sounds self-righteous and judgmental, especially if one were to talk of "holy people" or "saints." Nevertheless, if one pushes through these common misunderstandings into a deeper logic, then one has to deal with these very important claims: Of the many characteristics God is often associated with in the biblical testimony, one of the most predominant is that God is holy. Furthermore, God-fearers and God-followers are called to be holy as the Lord our God is

13. I am loosely drawing from the definition on offer by McClendon and Smith in *Convictions*, 5–6.

holy (Lev 19:2), meaning that holiness is not only a possibility for children of the promise but essentially a *commandment*. As Christians, then, when we say that we are called to follow Jesus, we mean that we are called to be disciples/followers/students of the Holy One of Israel. And in this following/formation, we are furthermore called to be like him. *To be Christ-like means to be holy*. Christians are called to be a holy people who demonstrate and embody God's holiness before a profane world.

What I have outlined above in terms of the development of convictions is nothing short of growing in holiness. When we are living into the call that God places upon our lives, we are growing closer to God and becoming more conformed to God's purposes. When this dynamic is occurring, we are being changed by the Spirit of God to become holy as God is holy. On the one hand, that is a terrifying thought. In obeying and following God, we are becoming God-like. It is easy for us to see the dangers of presumption and pride here. We have to wrestle constantly with the temptation of thinking too highly of ourselves, of begetting a "holier-than-thou" attitude that can harm ourselves and the cause of the gospel in the world. At the same time, too much is lost if we choose not to honor God's work in our lives by avoiding to call it what it is. Yes, it is strange, off-putting, and significantly ill-advised to claim before the world, "I am holy!" But at another level, it is equally wrong to avoid giving God the glory by choosing not to say, "God is shaping me in the ways of holiness so that I can live in accordance with God's holy purposes, all for the glory of God." That kind of commitment can come to pass within that moment of formation called the "college experience." At a Christian university or college, the ingredients and conditions are all there for God to transform and shape us.

Conclusion

What I have described so far will not necessarily happen by going through the motions at a Christian institution of higher learning.

Attending class, going to chapel, and living in the residence halls in no way guarantee that the aims of a Christian college experience will take root in one's life. Intentionality, desire, and some level of openness have to play a role. God wishes to be our one true delight, the one in whom we live, move, and have our being (Acts 17:28), but there is a real expectation at different moments within the biblical testimony that following Jesus is an active affair: We are to deny ourselves, take up our cross, and follow Jesus (Matt 16:24; Mark 8:34; Luke 9:23), meaning that we are to drop what we are doing (because we are compelled to do so by something/someone else), leave our comfort zones, and go wherever God leads. Doing so is scary; coming to college and leaving home can be terrifying. But the assurance we have as Christians is that we are not alone. Immanuel, God with us, has come and is coming again. We have been gifted with life, and we have been given opportunities to explore the possibilities for what God could do with our lives. Now the key questions become: What do we do with what we have been given? For what/whom do we live?

For those of you who are college students, may the following charge guide your experience: May the college experience be for you not just another hoop to go through or another rite of passage that you have to pass through so that you can get to bigger and better things. No, may the college experience be one in which you encounter and continue to be conformed to our holy God. In other words, may you learn to pursue holiness as a liberal art, as a way of life, in all that you do, in all that you are, and in all that you think. God expects and (more importantly) deserves nothing less.

2

Salvation on Display in a Holy Life

Daniel Castelo and Mark P. Stone

WHAT IS SALVATION? FOR many coming to a Christian college or university, the answer to this question is obvious: Salvation is what Jesus provides for us, an eternal hope that we will be forgiven of our sins and allowed to enjoy and be with God for ever. Such an understanding is faithful and true within Christian reflection, but it is also truncated and inadequate. Simply put, salvation concerns much more than forgiveness of sins, the assurance of God's grace, and eternal hope. Indeed, the entire biblical witness concerning what it means to be "saved" is surprisingly diverse. One of the striking features of the biblical vocabulary of salvation is its profound "earthiness." Rather than an exclusive focus on an individual's spirituality, salvation also implies that we are saved from oppressive nations, unjust socioeconomic structures, sickness, demonic oppression, and other arrangements contrary to God's kingdom.

Dealing with a Dominant Model

In many Christian circles, salvation is often spoken of in terms of justification by faith through grace alone. This phrasing was popularized by Protestantism, the traditions begun by individuals such as Martin Luther, John Calvin, and their associates and followers. This way of conceiving salvation was due in part to the perceived excesses associated with the Roman Catholic penitential system, one in which specific acts of varying number and degree were instituted in order that one could make restitution for one's sins. The penitential system was beneficial in the sense that it required intentional actions on behalf of the remorseful; in other words, they had to exercise their agency for the sake of their spiritual lives. Some would go so far as to say that they were attempting to "work out their salvation" as Paul encourages the Philippians to do (2:12). The disadvantage of the penitential system was that in practice it too easily accommodated a "works-righteousness" approach to salvation, that is, a view that we are largely in control of securing and sustaining our salvation. Eventually, individuals started to find this alternative as it was practiced to be both frightening and unacceptable on at least two scores. First, if we are in control of securing and sustaining our salvation, then we are burdened with a huge responsibility to make sure that we do enough and are good enough to be saved. And second, the penitential system fostered the tendencies of quantifying and commercializing God's grace when in fact grace is ultimately God's and not ours. This tendency to commodify salvation has the potential to foster a laissez-faire spirituality, one that assumes salvation is secure and so sees no need to seek its realization in one's own life (not to mention others' lives as well). Once we "own" salvation and put it in our pocket, so to speak, where do we locate the impulse to live in holiness?

When Protestants picked up the language of justification, they were harkening back to the biblical testimony, particularly the voice of Paul. The Apostle uses this language explicitly at important places in his letters, such as Romans 4–5 and Galatians 2–3. Because of its cognate with "justice," many people think of "justification" as a forensic or legal term and how it might work within a Western lawcourt. All of us have a basic sense of what happens in legal court proceedings: Cases are made, evidence is weighed, and verdicts are rendered. Once that verdict is read and given, the person is declared either guilty or innocent, thereby indicating that justice has been served. If such a context determines the primary locality for understanding justification language in the Bible, then the idea follows that we are before God the Father in a great tribunal where the evidence for innocence or guilt is weighed. Given that we all sin and fall short of the glory of God, we are declared guilty, and yet, God the Father provides a way forward so that we as human sinners can avoid the penalty of sin, and this way is the sacrificial work of Jesus. He suffers the consequences of sin so that we, in a gracious and happy exchange, can have eternal life.

The above model is quite predominant in certain Christian circles.[1] Not all Christians hold to it as a dominant model, but many do. When one includes the full range of Christians, including Roman Catholic and Eastern Orthodox believers, the model has varying levels of popularity within global Christianity. In fact, other models are much more predominant and helpful given differing ecclesial contexts.[2] For instance, the juridical model works well with Western accounts of jurisprudence, those that operate from a guilt-based orientation. Other societies (for instance, those that are more shame-based) would not find this model as compelling for elaborating the wonderful work that God has done on our behalf. Other biblical models and metaphors are useful, including the market, the temple, the battlezone, and others.[3]

---

1. We have used generalizations so far to speak of this model, but it should be noted that nuances do exist from time to time in its elaboration; some of these will be noted below.

2. Roland Chia notes that the term "justification" is not even mentioned once in the great doctrinal manual of the Eastern church, namely *De Fidei Orthodoxa* by John of Damascus; in Chia's view, the most ancient of soteriological images is probably "union." See "Salvation as Justification and Deification," 127–28.

3. A text that is helpful on this score is Green and Baker, *Recovering the Scandal of the Cross.*

Again, latitude is possible here since the Bible does not solely use juridical or legal terminology to frame salvation; it may be that many Christians find this language helpful and compelling, but it by no means is singular or primordial in the biblical witness. Perhaps one of the most difficult aspects of justification when understood in the forensic or legal sense is that it is significantly objective in nature. What is meant by "objective" here is that the model deals with our status or identity with respect to the law. If one were to recall the imagery, then the limit can be exposed in this way: After the cases are made and the evidence weighed, the final verdict determines the guilt or innocence of the person. However, it may be that the person is actually innocent rather than guilty (or vice versa) and that the verdict gets it wrong. In addition to being possibly mistaken, the verdict presents no guarantee that the situation will not happen again: Just because a person is declared innocent one day does not mean that the person is rehabilitated or changed. Simply put, when one's identity or status is being considered, that process is one step removed from the interiority or condition of the person. The person may be one thing, and the declared identity/condition may be another.

Salvation as Sanctification

It is a great blessing that the Bible has a number of images for salvation since one metaphor simply cannot do all the heavy-lifting of describing exhaustively and comprehensively how God is for us. Rather than being a weakness or limit, the diversity of the biblical testimony is actually quite helpful on this count.

In fact, given the different ways that even Paul uses the language of "justification" in his writings, a case can be made that the legal or forensic context is not enough "to do justice" to the term. At its most basic, the term "justification" in Paul means "to restore to right relationship." The last word is what exposes the legal or forensic model as insufficient, for "relationship" is tied both to status/identity and to interiority/being; it is both an inner/subjective and outer/objective term. Take for instance a primary human relationship, that of the parent-child. In being biological children of other people, we naturally have an identity or status because of that relationship; we pick up a genetic endowment and all that this implies (physical, psychological, and other kinds of features), and we may even adopt a surname and experience certain consequences because of this identity. With all these links, however, there are no guarantees that the parent and child will be in a "right relationship" since "relationship" does not simply refer to genetic endowment, names, or a legal standing; the term also refers to a dynamic reality that has to be lived out and embodied.

What Paul has in mind when he speaks about "justification" is not simply a declared status or identity but also an abiding reality; to use the language of the Old Testament, the term suggests being at peace (*shalom*) with God. And this dynamic reality implies that something changes not only to our status or identity but also to our very selves. The change has to be both outer and inner, objective and subjective. In other words, our being has to change in addition to our standing before God.

The heart of much of classic Protestant thinking on salvation—specifically Lutheranism[4]—has been centered on justification by faith through grace alone. As a gift of God's grace, we are given the faith to trust in the work of Christ for us on the cross, and we are thereby justified, acquitted of all charges. Does this mean that God, as judge, simply looks at humanity—obviously guilty of sin—and unconditionally accepts the unacceptable? Does God turn a blind eye to our guilt because God has been "paid off" by the blood of Jesus? Is it merely *as though* we are righteous, while in reality we are not? This has often been believed to

---

4. Important to note here is a distinction between Luther and Lutheranism, as the Finnish interpretation of Luther has helped expose participatory features of Luther's thought. For a helpful survey of these possibilities within Luther, see Marshall, "Justification as Declaration and Deification."

be the case with the reference to the "imputed righteousness" of Christ. But for this "happy exchange," as Luther puts it, to really be good news, it must effect real change in us here and now. Our salvific hope is not simply reserved for the future but invades our present lives. Yes, it is true that Christ's righteousness is imputed to us through justifying faith in him, yet this step is only the beginning of the Christian life. Wesley contends that "God *implants* righteousness in every one to whom he has *imputed* it."[5] When we receive the salvation of Christ we are not only saved *from* sin and wrath but also *for* a life of holiness. In another place Wesley argues: "And at the same time that we are justified, yea, in that very moment, *sanctification* begins. . . . There is a *real* as well as a *relative* change."[6] This dynamic is beautifully explored in the concept of *theosis*, or divinization.

Usually associated with the Eastern Orthodox tradition, *theosis* basically means "participation in the divine nature" (see 2 Pet 1:4). "This 'nature,' or divine life, permeates the being of humans like leaven permeates bread, in order to restore it to its original conditions as *imago Dei*,"[7] the image of God. Don't worry: it is not as though we become "gods" or are somehow absorbed into an inert mass of divinity. Rather, the distinction between Creator and creature is maintained while we are conformed to the image of the first true human: Jesus. This idea of *theosis* is nothing new to the Christian tradition. In the late second century, Irenaeus wrote: "Our Lord Jesus Christ . . . through his transcendent love, [became] what we are, that he might bring us to be even what he is himself."[8] In the early fourth century, Athanasius declared: "[The Word of God] assumed humanity that we might become God."[9] Even Luther demonstrates characteristics of this view:

5. Wesley, "The Lord Our Righteousness," 458.

6. Wesley, "The Scripture Way of Salvation," 158.

7. Mannermaa, "Justification and *Theosis*," 26.

8. *Against Heresies*, Book V, preface.

9. *On the Incarnation*, par. 54. Chia phrases this notion helpfully, calling it the "Irenaean-Athanasian exchange principle" ("Salvation as Justification and

"Put briefly, [God] fills us in order that everything that he is and everything he can do might be in us in all its fullness, and work powerfully, so that we might be divinized throughout."[10] We are justified by faith through grace, and Christ's righteousness is imputed to us, but the very real presence of Christ in us also causes us to become righteous and holy. Theologians have persistently made this claim. For instance, salvation and morality are connected so intimately in Wesley's theology that they can be spoken of synonymously,[11] and even Luther "typically refuses to distinguish between the question of salvation and the question of ethics."[12]

Salvation, then, is not to be conceived of only in the negative sense—saved *from* sin—but in a positive sense as well: saved *for* a life of holiness. Such a view envisions salvation as sanctification. Salvation is a participatory journey of divinization in which we as individuals are changed and thereby empowered as agents of change on the earth. What we are called to be and participate in is a new reality, one that Christians label "the kingdom of God."

The Gospel in the Flesh

What is fascinating to consider when speaking of the kingdom of God is that God chose to display this kingdom *in the life of a person*. Christians do not appeal to a Magna Carta, a Constitution, or some other document when they talk about the gospel; they do not refer to an idea, a philosophy, or some other intellectual construct when speaking of salvation. No, Christians appeal to a person and his life on earth as being the way, the truth, and the life for us (John 14:6). God's response to the theodicy question, God's gesture in light of all the decay, corruption, and death that we see all around us, is a humble man hailing from Nazareth.

Deification," 131).

10. As quoted in Peura, "What God Gives Man Receives," 92.

11. Long, *John Wesley's Moral Theology*, 163.

12. Peura, "What God Gives Man Receives," 78.

That God chose a human life to initiate and show the kingdom of God suggests that what God requires from us is a certain kind of life as well. God does not simply want our assent but our hearts, not just our words but our desires. But that is not all. Not only do Christians affirm that on display in Jesus' life is the truest and most compelling expression of who God is and what God is like, but they also claim that this life is the most genuine and truthful expression of what humanity is and what humanity is called to be. Jesus lived the one authentic human life. Jesus was human the way God always intended humanity to be. One senses this logic in both the New Testament and in the early patristic testimony when Christ is said to be a "Second Adam." Jesus lives a human life the way Adam should have. Christ "re-heads" or "recapitulates" human existence in his life, providing a "do-over," if you will, of what should have been the case all along. In making such a claim, we do not skirt over the brute reality of it all: Jesus suffered, was rejected, was betrayed, and underwent a premature, excessively harsh, and agonizing death. He lived the one authentic human life in the midst of inauthentic, corrupt, and fallen human existence. He was a Second Adam in the wake of the violent and cruel conditions resulting from the First Adam's downfall.

When we start to come to terms with these pressing matters, we realize part of the logic of why salvation has come to the world in the life of a human being. Through Jesus, we can catch a glimpse of what we are called to be, of what we were meant to be all-along. Salvation has come to us in the form of a life, and salvation is to be appropriated by us through a growing correspondence to that life in our own lives. Salvation is not a benefit; it is not the greatest insurance policy every devised— eternal security all for the low, low price of cognitive assent and verbal acceptance. No. If that is salvation, then it is a meager salvation, one that simply cannot account for just how bad we humans and our current lot can and tend to be. Salvation is a way of life, a way of being, a different kind of reality that we have been invited and blessed to participate in. This reality is transformative: it changes us from the inside out. Our living, moving, coming and going have to change qualitatively in a very real and detectable way when we come to faith. It is that serious; it ought to change everything.

So, can we do what Jesus did? No, we cannot save the world or conquer death; we cannot live a sinless life because we have sinned and continue to fail from time to time (and if you don't think you do, then, if we were you, we would worry about a little something called "pride"). *But we can begin to lead a life like his.* In fact, we are called to nothing less: We are to be holy/perfect as Jesus—the image of the Father—is holy/perfect. As Christians, we are called to follow Christ, and following means not simply to witness him doing all the heavy lifting of repairing and healing the world but to join in that work.

And this healing and repair of ourselves are realities that we participate in. God calls us out of the profane world to be his holy people. As God's holy people, we abide in God just as God abides in us. This "abiding" or "remaining" language is so crucial for thinking of the life of discipleship. As Jesus points out in the gospel of John, we are to abide in him just as he abides in the Father (John 15). We are called to participate, to abide and remain, in the holy life of God.

3

Holiness in the Old Testament

Kelsie Gayle Job and Frank Anthony Spina

WHAT FIRST COMES TO mind when hearing words like "holy" or "holiness?" Marked religious sensitivity? A serene piety? Profound spiritual depth? Uncompromising morality? Steadfast integrity? These possibilities and others of their ilk underscore the fact that we tend to regard holiness as religion in its most concentrated and loftiest form. Holiness is religion on steroids! Indeed, so much is this the case that holiness comes close to having an otherworldly aura. This explains why we almost automatically think of God as holy—God is virtually the personification of holiness.

Though certainly not on par with God, we may even grant that human beings are capable of being holy as well. But we typically consider holy folk to be extremely rare. Somehow, they are not like the rest of us. These are "saints," after all, who are honored with special feast days in the church, are depicted on stained glass windows, have medals or statues to commemorate their achievements, or are lauded for having gone over and above the call of standard religious duty. We think of them as having written Gospels (Saint Matthew, Saint Luke), performed miracles, become popes, founded movements, or lived ascetic lives in monasteries. Though we ordinary folk may be serious about our Christian faith, even given to prayer and assorted acts of service, we are under little illusion that we will ever belong to the company of the saints.

But is that a valid sentiment? Is such a resigned attitude warranted, however respectful of God and God's apparently few saintly stalwarts? As it turns out, believing that holiness is only for a few special people not only betokens a kind of false humility, but it is plainly wrong from a biblical standpoint. As a matter of fact, leaving aside for a moment serious biblical exploration, consider how certain common sentiments belie the idea that holiness is so exalted a state that it is beyond ordinary people. Everyday language indicates that at least at a popular level holiness is much more down to earth and part of the ebb and flow of everyday life than one might initially think. For instance, people often blurt out "holy cow" or "holy smokes" at moments of incredulity or shock.

Now, before dismissing such usage as mere rhetorical flourish bearing no particular theological or religious weight, we have to realize that these expressions—and many others just like them—accord in some sense with the biblical use of the noun "holiness" (*qōdeš*), the adjective "holy" (*qādôš*), and the verb "make holy/sanctify/consecrate" (*qiddēš*). When it comes to biblical teaching, clearly holiness is a function of a sovereign, transcendent God who is wholly Other. At the same time, as we shall see, holiness may characterize the most mundane of objects; various times, days, or seasons; rituals; and even people.

A Holy God

As intimated, any discussion of holiness in the Old Testament (or the entire Christian Bible for that matter) begins—and ultimately ends—with God, whom the great prophet Isaiah referred to often as the Holy One of Israel.[1] The Old Testament deity (YHWH[2]) is holy in essence; anything else that is holy—and there is no limit to what may be made holy, or sanctified—is holy as a result of direct divine action or proximity to this holy God. Few texts capture the awesome and fulsome nature of God as utterly holy better than Isaiah 6:1–3, a vision in which God is pictured sitting "high and lifted up" on a royal throne surrounded by seraphim, magnificent heavenly attendants of God, who intone to one another:

> Holy, holy, holy is the Lord of hosts; the whole earth is full of His glory.

The reaction to this incredible depiction of God, involving not only the prophet himself but the surrounding world, is precisely what one would expect. Being in the presence of a holy deity is simultaneously awe-inspiring, humbling, and, yes, even frightening. Holiness underscores God's greatness, majesty, and power. In this context God is not to be managed, domesticated, or discussed but submitted to and worshipped. All holiness, wherever found and however implemented, is derivative of this sovereign deity.

Holiness is not something God acquires or merely exhibits. Holiness is part of the essence of God. Odd as it seems, little logic is supplied to argue that God is holy. God is holy because God is God. That is merely the fact of the matter. God is not holy because God is just, love, powerful, or gracious. God is holy because God is. No other explanation is required or ever given. In a way, God is holy "just because."

In this light, it is no accident that God's holiness and God's glory (*kābōd*) are tandem realities. Glory is difficult to define. The nuance of the noun is that glory is substantial, weighty, and

1. See, for instance, Isaiah 1:4; 5:19, 24; 10:20; 12:6; 17:7; 30:11, 12, 15; 31:1; 37:23; 41:14; 43:3, 14; 45:11; 47:4; 48:17; 54:5; and 60:14.

2. This name, the Tetragrammaton, is the one revealed to Moses at the burning bush (Exodus 3). Sometimes, individuals add vowels to the consonants for how they think it was pronounced; we prefer to follow the standard Hebrew practice out of reverence.

overwhelming. It is sometimes associated with thick smoke, spectacular weather, or clouds. In a sense, glory signifies the presence of God in concentrated form. We have already noted the juxtaposition of God's holiness and God's glory in Isaiah 6, in which the three-fold repetition of "holy, holy, holy" on the part of the seraphim is parallel to the whole earth being full of divine glory (v. 3). Subsequently, the temple itself felt the effects of this collective intonation while the (holy) building filled with smoke (v. 4). The prophet was at that point only able to respond with abject humility and a confession of sin (v. 5). The holy, glorious presence of God is overpowering.

Key Old Testament Examples

Another instance where holiness and glory are associated is the scene when Solomon is about to dedicate the finished temple in Jerusalem. At the appropriate moment, the priests emerge from *the holy place*—indicating a special part of the temple wherein the divine presence is concentrated—whereupon a cloud symbolizing the glory of God fills the whole temple. As the priests are engulfed by the divine presence, so to speak, they "could not stand to minister" (1 Kgs 8:10–11; see also 2 Chr 5:11, 13–14). Few "properties" are more expressive of an encompassing divine presence than divine holiness and glory. Whether in the form of smoke or a cloud, we begin to get a completely different idea about "holy smoke(s)!" through these depictions. There is a reason the church has often used incense to evoke the intense presence of a holy God.

The ark story in First Samuel also combines God's holiness and God's glory in an important manner. In this episode Israel tries to insure victory after an initial defeat at the hand of the Philistines. They do this by bringing into battle the Ark of the Covenant, believed to contain the divine presence (1 Sam 4:1–5); however, the ploy failed. Adding insult to injury, the Ark was captured and taken away for some time (4:11; 6:1). One of the

responses to this tragic turn of events was the birth of a baby to the wife of Phineas, one of the priests killed during the battle (4:11, 19). The mother, who died soon after the birth, named her baby Ichabod, a name likely meaning "inglorious." Before she dies, the mother explains this odd naming as follows: "The glory has departed from Israel, for the ark of God has been captured" (4:21–22). In this instance, God's presence and God's glory are taken to be one and the same.

But that is not the end of the story. Ironically, in this account both the Israelites and the Philistines discover in different ways that neither the glory of God nor the holiness of God are to be trifled with. The Philistines learn their lesson when they find out that the God whom they thought they had subdued not only made a mockery out of their own god, Dagon, but devastated their land as well (1 Sam 5:1–10). Phineas's wife had lamented that the glory had departed Israel, but it turns out that the glory was alive and well in the land of the Philistines. Before long, the Philistines could not move fast enough to return to Israel the Ark, now seen to be alive with the dangerous presence of God (5:11—6:16).

However, Israel was no more immune to the divine presence than the Philistines had been. When the Ark returns to Israel—to Bethshemesh to be exact—a number of men looked into it and were slain by the Lord. The irony of this action is that Israel might have been thinking that God was not present after their ignominious defeat by the Philistines. But the whole point of the story is that God is not "in the box" when one demands it but is often present when presumed to be absent. When Israel discovers to its horror that God was "in the box," leading to an alarming swift judgment, the survivors respond, "Who is able to stand before the Lord (YHWH), this holy God?" Clearly, holiness in this case was anything but welcoming. This biblical moment is an instance where the glory and holiness of God were on display in a powerful and fearful way. In some situations, the glory and holiness of God not only prompt an appropriate fear but underscore the radical difference between God and God's creatures.

Given this particular feature of holiness, it might seem counterintuitive that this same holy God has no trouble sanctifying other things, even profane objects.

Sacred Time

Indeed, this disposition is seen immediately in the strategic narrative of God's creation of "the heavens and the earth" (Gen 1:1; 2:1). As is well known, the Genesis creation story portrays creation taking place over the span of six days, each consisting equally of an "evening and a morning." Only the seventh day was not a day designated for divine creative activity; that day was not just "another day," so to speak. Just as God blessed elements in the created order (1:22, 28), so God also blessed the seventh day (2:3). But God does something else besides bless this day: God also sanctifies it (2:3), setting it apart as a day of divine rest and later as a day of rest for all God's people (Exod 20:8). Here we observe God's ability to sanctify time, that is, setting it apart for a purpose in accord with God's agenda.

Holy Things

The same holds true for objects as well. Virtually anything may be transformed by God's sanctifying power into something holy. One finds within the biblical testimony such examples as holy ground (Exod 3:5), a holy city (Isa 48:2; 52:1 [Jerusalem]), a holy temple (1 Chron 29:3), a holy ark (2 Chron 35:3), holy chambers (Ezek 42:13), holy mountains or hills (Jer 31:23), holy garments (Exod 28:2, 4), holy crowns (Exod 29:6), holy tunics (Lev 16:4), holy vessels or pots (1 Sam 21:5), holy bread (1 Sam 21:6), holy sacrifices (Exod 29:27), and holy water (Num 5:17). The list could go on, for there is nothing which God cannot sanctify.

Divine action of this sort may be understood in sacramental terms. A sacrament is a "means of grace" whereby God makes special use of something ordinary and profane for extraordinary and sacral purposes. One thinks in this context of the Eucharist, whereby plain bread and wine are consecrated by God so that they become mysteriously and miraculously the body and blood of the Lord Jesus Christ. Such sacramental thinking is deeply rooted in the Old Testament's lavish presentation of God's ability to sanctify any and all material forms. There is nothing that is ultimately *secular*—ostensively an area in which God is absent— since every part of the created order is susceptible to being sanctified by God for God's own purposes.

Being and Doing

By now it takes no stretch of the imagination to realize that people, too, are sanctified by God. Thus, it hardly needs mentioning that priests may be considered holy (Exod 28:3). However, beyond any individual who might engage in sacerdotal activities at God's behest and in service to God's people (as important as that dimension surely is), the presentation of the elect people of God as collectively holy deserves yet greater emphasis. God's elect community, whose ancestors are called in Genesis 12—50 and who enter later into covenant relationship with God after being rescued from Egypt (Exodus), is without ambiguity referred to as a holy nation (*goy qādôš*) as well as a kingdom of priests (Exod 19:6). In this case, Israel as the elect people of God is holy because—and only because—she has been specially chosen by God as a light to the nations and as instrumental in God's redeeming, restoring, and reconciling the whole created order. Given this divine initiative, Israel does not need to *try* to be holy; the community is already holy by virtue of God's selection, which is a function of lavish divine grace and an inscrutable divine will. This idea is matched in the New Testament by the practice of referring to the members of the church as "holy ones," that is, saints (*hagioi*).[3]

However, in spite of the fact that Israel is holy by virtue of its divine call by a holy deity (Deut 7:6; 14:2), the members of this community are continually admonished to be holy (Deut 26:19; 28:9). This call means that in every aspect of its common life together, Israel is to act out her holy calling to be the people of God. The admonition for God's people, who are already in one sense holy, to act in a holy manner before God involves the full range of behaviors befitting their calling. Such activity could involve food (Lev 11:44; 24:9), cleanliness (Deut 23:15), the ordination of priests (Lev 21:6–8), sex (Lev 20:10–16), or any other activity. Positively, Israel is to comport itself in every circumstance and situation in a manner that accords with the holy God who formed the community in the first place. Negatively, Israel is to refrain from any activity which would besmirch God's holy name. An individual's membership in this holy community calls for holy living because each one is beholden to the community as a whole. This holy ethic is summed up well in Leviticus: "You (i.e. Israel) shall be holy to me; for I the Lord am holy, and I have separated you from the other peoples to be mine" (20:26).

The Biblical Call as a Whole

This pan-biblical admonition for Israel to be holy even though they are already holy by virtue of divine election is akin to the admonitions in the New Testament letters to the churches. Because the recipients of the letters are already members of the church, the Body of Christ, they are in fact holy. Yet, all the letters contain exhortations to these various communities to conduct their lives in a manner that is consistent with their calling in Jesus Christ. In effect, these saints are being exhorted to live a saintly life. They are to be saints not only formally but materially as well. The same

3. Instances here include Rom 1:7; 1 Cor 1:2; 2 Cor 1:1; Eph 1:1; Phil 1:1; Col 1:2).

holy deity who called the community of faith—Israel and by extension the church—supplies the grace necessary for a holy life on the part of its constituent members. Like Israel, the church is a holy nation and a kingdom of priests.

The accent on the elect people of God as holy also brings into bold relief the most important thing God's people do: worship. All service, every ministry, every act of compassion, and every expression of love are rooted in and derivative of the people's worship. The most appropriate response to a holy God is holy worship. For this reason, the Old Testament emphasizes holy days, holy ceremonies, holy rites, holy personnel, holy places, and holy objects. Israel acknowledges its election and mission when it worships through its sacred liturgy the God without whom it would not exist or have purpose.

Conclusion

Holiness is central to the Old Testament. A holy God elected a people and set them apart to lead a holy life for the purpose of restoring, redeeming, and reconciling the whole created order. Holiness is not optional, for being a part of the elect community means that God's sanctifying power has already been at work. We are already saints. But that is not a point of pride, for we are saints by virtue of God's grace. Now, it is incumbent upon us to participate in the elect community—through holy worship, a holy life, holy service and ministry—so that our common life together is a sacramental reminder that we were initially called and consecrated by the Holy One of Israel.

4

"And Ever Toward Each Other Move"

Holiness as a Communal Reality

Douglas M. Koskela

CAN WE BE HOLY apart from the church? The question may strike some people as strange, especially those who have had painful experiences in the church. Too often, people honestly seeking hope, grace, and genuine community have bravely ventured into a local congregation only to find cold faces and a feeling of exclusion. In other cases, those who have faithfully served the church for years come to find that their efforts are unappreciated or even criticized. If holiness involves being set apart for a particular way of life in line with God's purposes, then it is sometimes difficult to see in a faith community that often looks all too much like the surrounding world. We might be tempted to wonder if we have the question backward: Should we be asking if it's possible to be holy *in* the church?

In this light, we might be quite surprised by one of the confessions made in the third article of the Apostles' Creed: It is the *church* that is confessed to be holy. Most of us are familiar with the call to personal holiness, no matter how difficult we might find its fulfillment. But the idea that holiness relates to the church is somewhat novel to many people. And given the disappointment with the church noted above, we might initially resist the idea that holiness is a communal reality. It is precisely this connection that must be engaged, however, if we are truly to embody holiness in a Christian key. How can we flesh out the church as a locus of holiness? What might it mean to think of holiness as a communal reality? I would suggest that three things come to the fore in this discussion: 1) the church is the context in which personal holiness is fostered; 2) the church reflects holiness in its corporate life; and 3) the church testifies to God's holiness in its worship.

The Church as the Context of Personal Holiness

It is important to acknowledge right up front that the Christian life cannot be lived adequately on one's own. Though each of us is accountable to God for our thoughts, habits, and choices, none of us is expected to pursue holiness in isolation. As N. T. Wright so vividly remarks, "It is as impossible, unnecessary, and undesirable to be a Christian all by yourself as it is to be a newborn baby all by yourself."[1] Just as a newborn requires the nurturing of its caregivers, so also our growth and maturity in the Christian life depends on the support, accountability, and guidance of the community of faith. In the contemporary setting, it has become quite common for people to attempt to "go it alone" in the Christian faith by substituting personal devotional times or prayerful hikes in the woods for active participation in a local congregation. To a great extent, this inclination is quite understandable given the frustrations that so many have had with the church. However, not only does this approach to the Christian life detach key devotional practices such as prayer and reading Scripture from the broader context in which they were meant to function,

1. Wright, *Simply Christian*, 210.

but it also proves how extraordinarily difficult it is to sustain such practices alone over the long haul.

One person who recognized this all too well was the eighteenth century English revivalist John Wesley. He put this point quite sharply: "Christianity is essentially a social religion . . . to turn it into a solitary religion is indeed to destroy it."[2] When Wesley and his fellow leaders in the Methodist movement sought to "spread Scriptural holiness across the land," they developed a vast network of accountability structures.[3] Wesley and his partners in ministry recognized that the accountability, encouragement, and mutual prayer support of committed small groups were essential for cultivating holiness. In those "class meetings" and "bands," members did not simply gather for casual conversation. They asked each other tough, direct questions about their spiritual condition in a context of love and mutual commitment. What was true in Wesley's day is no less true today: We simply need each other if we are to be shaped in the likeness of Christ. And this is not limited to small group accountability, as valuable and important as such structures are. Life in the local congregation is aimed "to provoke one another to love and good deeds" (Heb 10:24). By gathering together, worshiping, sharing in the sacraments, reading Scripture together—ultimately, by sharing our lives with each other—we are shaped in the way of holiness.

Two features of our current historical context, however, work against our appreciation for the church as the natural home for cultivating sanctity. First, the rugged individualism of modern (and particularly North American) culture leads us to resist any notion of dependence on others as we move toward ultimate goals. The story of the determined individual who "made it" against all odds despite the widespread doubts of others is a cultural paradigm with tremendous romantic appeal. Acknowledgment of neediness or dependence, on the other hand, carries

2. Wesley, "Upon Our Lord's Sermon on the Mount, Discourse 4," 533.

3. For a historical account of the early Methodist movement and its structures, see Heitzenrater, *Wesley and the People Called Methodists*.

little romantic appeal. Second, a deep suspicion of institutions is prevalent in our cultural discourse.[4] The idea that what we genuinely need might be offered in something as blatantly institutional as the church runs afoul of contemporary sensibilities. Despite the fact that there is an institutional dimension to just about any sustained and meaningful social gathering, this suspicion emerges very commonly in discussions on the importance of the church.

Such factors need not dislodge our pursuit of holiness from its natural context. In fact, a healthy community of believers depending on God and on each other in the maturing of their faith might speak all the more to a culture averse to dependence. And such a community is the very antidote for the viral individualism that threatens our ongoing development in the body of Christ. Jonathan S. Raymond refers to this as the "social ecology" of holiness: "In the social ecology of holiness, our Lord continues to restore and develop us in holiness and Christ-likeness. He continues to complete that which he intended from the beginning."[5] Furthermore, beyond our need for the communal context of our own pursuit of holiness, each of us has particular gifts to contribute to the community of faith. The charisms given by the Holy Spirit are not ultimately for our own personal edification but rather for the building up of the body of Christ. Withholding our particular contribution because we don't feel the need for the church effectively deprives others of the gifts we have to share. Our focus too often is on what we might or might not get from the church, but we do well also to ask what we might give. Finally, one last reason to push back against the idea of "free agent" Christianity has to do with the very nature of the church. Not only is the church a gathering of those who have been called and set apart by God, but it also is a sign of God's salvific work. The church visibly models the reconciling work of Jesus, which

4. An excellent treatment of this issue is offered in Heclo, *On Thinking Institutionally.*

5. Raymond, "Social Holiness," 179.

leads naturally to our discussion of the conspicuous sanctity of the church itself.

Holiness in the Corporate Life of the Church

Given the discussion up to this point, one might be inclined to conclude that the church is only important in its role of fostering *personal* holiness. There is, however, much more to the communal dimension of sanctity. When we confess the holiness of the church, we are not only confessing the instrumental role of the community in shaping personal holiness. In some sense, we are also confessing that the community itself reflects what it means to be holy. As a sign of God's reconciling work in Jesus Christ, the church both displays and participates in God's transformation of creation. A central dimension of that transforming work is the healing of human relationships. If enmity and isolation reflect the disordering of creation, then the work of salvation is not complete as long as it is confined to the sphere of the individual. The breaking down of social barriers, the hard work of genuine forgiveness, and the cultivation of shared life together all manifest the saving work of God. And to a society largely unaccustomed to these dynamics, the power of such witness can be startling.

The world saw a vivid example of what communal holiness looks like in October of 2006. In Lancaster County, Pennsylvania, a gunman held a number of students hostage in a one-room Amish schoolhouse, eventually shooting and killing five of them before taking his own life. It is not difficult to imagine how most communities would respond to such an act of violence. Yet this particular Amish community startled the watching world by reaching out in concrete acts of forgiveness and love to the family of the shooter. Members of the community visited the shooter's family repeatedly, offering words of comfort for *their* loss. The community even started a charitable fund to support the practical needs of the shooter's children.

Much of the media coverage of the tragedy focused on the Amish response, precisely because it was so unexpected. If holiness means being distinct from the patterns and practices that are common in the world for the purpose of embracing that world in reconciling love, then this response demonstrated that a community can indeed reflect holiness.[6]

How might such a community be formed? Anyone with even the slightest experience in the church can vouch that holiness is not an immediate or automatic result of responding to the gospel. On the other hand, we might tend to balk at the idea that communal sanctity is developed over time by means of particular practices that form our habits. The reason for such hesitation is that the work of transformation is rightly attributed to God—specifically, to the work of the Holy Spirit. If it is indeed God who forms a community in holiness, some may ask why God should need time and repetition to accomplish this work. But this question reflects a rather truncated doctrine of the Holy Spirit. There is little ground for supposing that the Spirit must work immediately or directly in accomplishing any divine purpose (even as we fully acknowledge the freedom of the Holy Spirit to do just that). On the contrary, the role of the means of grace in the life of the church suggests a very different vision of the Spirit's work. The divine calling to gather in eucharistic fellowship, to meditate together on the scriptures, to pray fervently and consistently, and to engage in acts of mercy make it clear that God works *in and through* these very practices to shape holy communities. We need not choose between God's agency and human practices in cultivating ecclesial sanctity when we recognize that such practices are ordinary means of God's action. We can affirm boldly, then, that it is the Holy Spirit that forms such communities even as we engage in concrete practices that serve as the channels of holy formation.

---

6. For one account of the tragedy and its aftermath, see Kraybill, Nolt, and Weaver-Zercher, *Amish Grace*.

In this light, a deep commitment to habit formation must be in place before crisis situations (such as the Amish community faced) emerge. Shaped by a longstanding pattern of training in holy living, the church will be prepared to face whatever situations it may encounter. Samuel Wells offers a substantial account of such practices in his book *Improvisation*. He writes: "Training requires commitment, discipline, faithfulness, study, apprenticeship, practice, cooperation, observation, reflection—in short, moral effort. The point of this effort is to form skills and habits—habits that mean people take the right things for granted and skills that give them ability to do the things they take for granted."[7] Just as an Olympic athlete might spend hundreds of hours over many years preparing for a few minutes of competition, so also the community of faith is trained in the patterns of holiness by means of disciplined commitment. (And again, this analogy should not obscure the fact that the actual power of formation is that of the Holy Spirit.) Wells continues by highlighting worship as the central means of training: "Thus in worship Christians seek in the power of the Spirit to be conformed to the image of Christ—to act like him, think like him, and be like him."[8] When we are inclined to doubt that such transformation is possible, therefore, we have two responses ready at hand. The first is to remember always that it is by God's saving power that our ecclesial practices have their desired effect. The second is, by God's grace, to get to work—namely, the very particular "work of the people" that is Christian worship.

The Holiness of God and the Church's Worship

It must be said, finally, that not even the most poignant examples of holy communities define what holiness is. Rather, we are called to holiness because of God's holiness. An essential way in which

7. Wells, *Improvisation*, 75.
8. Ibid., 84.

we live out that calling is in our worship. The church's liturgical practices not only enable us to recognize and affirm God's holiness, but they also draw us toward that holiness.

John Webster suggests that in the act of confessing the holy God "is manifest the basic character of the Church's holiness, for, in the act of confession, the Church joins with the prophets and apostles and martyrs, all those whose lives have been transfigured by the divine calling, and becomes that human company which is holy in its confession of this one, the Lord God of hosts."[9] Human beings tend to become gradually more like that which they adore, and thus the church casts its adoring gaze upon the holy God in anticipation of its own transfiguration.

What, specifically, does the confession of God's holiness entail? Ultimately, both God's distinction from the world *and* God's embrace of the world serve as the paradigm of holiness. While some accounts of God's holiness emphasize *only* the notion of otherness, a trinitarian account of holiness will also emphasize the divine initiative in making Godself known to creation. The God who is present in the incarnate Son and in the Holy Spirit always remains "other"—such is the nature of God's holiness. This affirmation of both God's immanence and God's transcendence is emphasized by Hans Urs von Balthasar: "As the 'holy one,' God makes known especially his divinity in its supramundane character separated from the world; as the 'glorious one,' he makes known both his 'being present' in the world and, united to this, his sovereign superiority to the world."[10] When our thinking, praying, and singing neglect God's transcendence, we all too easily tend toward idolatry. And idolatry need not involve a rival god of some sort; common theological tendencies to "domesticate" God (however

---

9. Webster, *Holiness*, 66.

10. Von Balthasar, *The Glory of the Lord*, 7:268. While von Balthasar *distinguishes* between God's holiness and God's glory, he insists that these attributes cannot be *separated*.

unwittingly) amount to the same problem.[11] On the other hand, when we miss God's radical and particular immanence in the economy of salvation, we distort our vision of holiness into a generic philosophical concept. A trinitarian vision of holiness, in other words, is intimately connected to the particular work of this God in history "for us and for our salvation."

Such a recognition leads us inevitably to worship. Indeed, part of what Christian worship is about is witnessing to and celebrating the holiness of God. We rejoice together not only that God loves the world enough to do so but also that God transcends the world and thus is *able* to work toward its salvation. Testifying in worship to this dual affirmation of God's holiness is a central part of the church's calling. When we gather to worship Father, Son, and Holy Spirit, we tell and retell the narrative of salvation in the reading of Scripture, the singing of hymns, the partaking of sacraments, and preaching. This point is made vividly by Marva J. Dawn: "We who live by the name *Christian* are those rescued from ourselves by the salvation wrought by Jesus. Since salvation is entirely God's gift and not deserved or earned, Christian worship above all makes clear who is the giver of that and every other gift and challenges the world to respond to who he is."[12] In light of the earlier affirmation that the church's practices of worship are the primary means by which the Holy Spirit forms a community in holiness, the content of those practices is absolutely essential. If we are to be shaped in accordance with the holiness of the triune God, then the particular words we say and the concrete actions we take matter a great deal. Thus our prayers, songs, sacraments, and common life should both acknowledge God's distinction from the world and invoke God's continuing embrace of the world.

In these three ways, then—forming personal holiness, forming corporate holiness, and witnessing together to the

---

11. This tendency in modern Christian theology is addressed in Placher, *The Domestication of Transcendence*.

12. Dawn, *Reaching Out without Dumbing Down*, 76.

triune God—holiness involves the whole community of faith. We should not allow these three to be separated. For our collective practices of fostering personal holiness and our communal practices that reflect holiness are ultimately acts of worship, testifying to the holiness of the triune God. As was so often the case, it was the pen of Charles Wesley that gave vivid expression to this reality. In his hymn "Jesus, United by Thy Grace," the younger Wesley recognized our movement toward God as a movement toward each other. May his prayer be ours:

> Jesu, united by thy grace, and each to each endeared, With confidence we seek thy face, and know our prayer is heard/Touched by the lodestone of thy love, let all our hearts agree, and ever toward each other move, and ever move toward thee.[13]

13. "Hymn 490," 677–78.

5

Participatory Holiness

A New Testament Perspective[1]

Robert W. Wall

ACCORDING TO THE NICENE Creed, Christians confess they belong to "one, *holy*, catholic and apostolic church." They make this bold claim not in arrogant attribution of their own moral superiority but in faithful acknowledgement that the church is made so by a holy God. God declares believers these things because they choose to trust in Christ's work for their salvation from sinfulness and then depend upon his Spirit to empower their lives to enter into God's presence for worship and praise.

For this reason, Paul can rightly address readers of First Corinthians as "holy ones" (*hagioi*). The Apostle does so not because he assumes their exemplary life but because they belong to a community that has been "sanctified (*hagiazo*) in Christ Jesus" (1 Cor 1:2). The central character of his narrative of salvation is God who has graciously entered into a covenant partnership with people marked out by faith in Christ and are declared by God "a holy (*hagios*) nation" (Exod 19:6; 1 Pet 2:9). In fact, God's

1. I acknowledge with gratefulness the collaboration of my student Mr. Raoul Perez in writing this chapter.

initial declaration of a wayward Israel's holiness on Mount Sinai is rooted in the very same theological soil as Paul's address of a sanctified congregation in his first letter to Corinthian Christians whose life is rife with internal conflict, moral laxity, theological confusion and spiritual immaturity. Saints?! Surely not!

Despite our reservations, sainthood is conferred by God not in fair-minded recognition of our practiced holiness but as an act of sheer grace. Any discussion of a biblical theology of holiness must begin with God and with a people whom a loving God regards as "one, holy, catholic and apostolic" as an act of mercy and not merit. Otherwise most people would find it difficult to take the Nicene confession of a holy church seriously, since it contradicts its routine experience of moral and spiritual failure. Read the newspapers, people!! When asked to explain the church's self-professed claim of holiness, most of us shrug our shoulders and explain that it must be true only in the abstract. The church is legally but not practically holy; holiness is a status conferred by God in some heavenly transaction that only God finds convincing. We may even suppose that the church's experience with holiness occurs only when it rubs up against a holy God in worship. Holiness is surely not a practice, a lifestyle; it's not really something we do or are. The church is holy by grace through faith—and we might hastily add, "not of works lest anyone boast!"

Why, then, is Scripture so pointed and persistent in asking the impossible of us: to be "holy in all our conduct" because the God we worship is holy (Lev 19:2; 1 Pet 1:15–16)? How does the biblical imperative to grow into the likeness of a holy God help guide (rather than frustrate) the hard choices ordinary Christians must make to mark their lives as faithful disciples of Jesus? This essay provides no easy answers because Scripture doesn't. Its purpose is to help readers (whose experiences may be counterintuitive to this sacred calling) construct a realistic vision of Christian life that underscores the practical importance of making hard and sometimes costly choices to live holy lives in the midst of a pervasively unholy, post-Christian world.

The Scriptural Logic of Covenant-Keeping

Let's begin this study with an interpretive rule that guides all serious approaches to biblical interpretation: The student enters the often strange world of Scripture through a gate built by the Old Testament narrative of salvation. In fact, the prophetic rubrics we use to distinguish the two parts of Scripture's story of God's Gospel, "old" and "new," imply an important truth about their close working relationship: Scripture's first testament is made "old" (but not obsolete) because of what is found "new" in the second testament because of Jesus. That is, no third testament to God's saving activity is needed to complete this biblical drama of divine love. Moreover, the old and new testaments that make up the church's scripture are of a piece. Nothing that has become "new" because of Jesus overturns what has been made "old" because of him. Rather, read together as parts of a mutually-informing whole, the story of a faithful Jesus climaxes and completes the story of an often unfaithful Israel in a way that creates a fully biblical understanding of Christian existence.

If the Bible interpreter obeys this rule, two core beliefs frame a "new" testament teaching of holiness that are put into play by an "old" testament story of Israel. First, Israel's God is a holy God whose "hands-on" activity makes all things holy. God's election of Israel as a "treasured possession" relocates a particular people within the bounds of a covenant relationship with this holy God. As a result, Israel is made holy by God's own choosing (Exod 19:5–6). Second, maintaining this covenant relationship with a holy God requires that Israel also make a set of hard choices to be holy even as God is holy (Lev 19:2). Covenant-keeping is holy business! And God who elects Israel does not do all the heavy-lifting required for Israel to make this partnership work and its promise of blessing viable. God's gracious covenant-making decision rather obligates Israel's obedient covenant-keeping actions if this relationship is to have legs for a future with God (see Josh 23—24).

The deep logic of covenant-keeping is wonderfully expressed by Israel's annual observance (and so reminder) known as the Day of Atonement: God alone forgives and sanctifies Israel on this Day (Lev 16). While God's atonement and cleansing of the entire community from all its impurity is an act of sheer grace, its practical effect is that the sanctified community must now live a sanctified life for all to see (Lev 17—26). Atonement not only makes people holy; it obligates them to live in a holy way. This old story of biblical Israel is the church's story; Israel's annual Day of Atonement has been enacted anew and "once for all" by the cruciform Christ (Heb 9—10) so that his community of disciples, the Israel of God, is able to live holy lives as a testimony of God's salvation-creating grace. And the corporate shape of covenant-making, in which God's cleansing and transforming grace targets an entire community, reminds us that the life of personal holiness is much too demanding and costly to go it alone (see Eph 2:11–22). We need one another in loving support (see 1 Pet 1:22), and we especially need the means of grace that are distributed and received within this community to empower a long obedience in God's direction.

Let me repeat my initial points because it is foundational for everything else: By faith the church has already been sanctified by God. Scripture's Pauline witness in particular teaches us that the risen Christ has already poured out the holy Spirit to cleanse and transform those who believe in waters of regeneration (Titus 3:4–6). But surrounding this magnificent Pauline confession of faith is an extensive list of moral and social virtues (Titus 3:1–3) that reminds faithful readers of God's expectation that "good works" follow after an experience of God's saving grace (Titus 2:14; 3:8). If we are sanctified by grace through faith alone (that is, through our faith in God's faithfulness), then its practical effect in real life is to live a holy life in every nook and cranny of human existence—social/public and spiritual/personal. No exceptions. The dynamic effect of experiencing God's grace, which Paul calls "power," is not something hidden from view. Moreover, it is the public practice of Christ-likeness which establishes a criterion that confirms those who are indeed forgiven and sanctified by God's grace through faith in Christ. The differing shapes of personal holiness witnessed by Scripture suggest that there is no one-size-fits-all. God issues a general call to a holy life, but its particular demands are adaptable to one's own world and within the bounds of one's own sense of vocation (2 Tim 1:9). Yes, every Christian is implored to pursue a holy life in response to God's loving embrace, but what this looks like on the ground varies between time-zones and job descriptions.

But there's still another important point to score. Among Wesley's canonical sermons is one titled "The Almost Christian" in which he makes an important distinction between the "heathen honesty" of the "almost Christian" and the saving faith of the "altogether Christian."[2] He argues that a non-believer can live a life of moral virtue and religious practice, marked out by a "form of godliness," without ever experiencing the power of God's indwelling Spirit (see 2 Tim 3:5). The morally scrupulous life of the "almost Christian" does not save him unless it springs from a sincere faith in Christ and is led by God's Spirit (Rom 8:2–17). What more is needed is the saving faith of an "altogether Christian" that inspires and grounds the practices of a holy life as the fruit of genuine repentance.

Wesley's important distinction between saving faith, which *gains* believers favor with God, and the fruit of genuine repentance, which *retains* God's favor forever, is also a useful reminder. While personal holiness apart from saving faith does not work, neither does saving faith apart from holiness. Trading on a gospel saying in which Jesus demands both repentance (and so its self-evident fruit) and faith in the proclaimed gospel (so Mark 1:15), Wesley conceives of a much more robust conception of

2. See "The Almost Christian," 131–41.

holiness than the mere practice of a morally virtuous life. Rather, the practice of a fully biblical expression of holiness is grounded in the firm confidence that our salvation from sin and our capacity to live a holy life result from Christ's atoning death and victorious resurrection. This, Wesley claims, is the holiness of the "altogether Christian" whose holy life is the measure of God's love shed abroad in a heart made receptive by placing confidence in what Christ has already done.

Not "This or That" but "This and That"

Some Christians, especially Protestants whose religious sensibilities are cultivated primarily at Scripture's Pauline address (and its main residence, with Luther, at Romans and Galatians), may reasonably suppose that holy living "just happens" by grace as though by a kind of spiritual osmosis: sanctification is by God's grace through faith alone, not good works lest we boast in ourselves rather than in God. Some actually believe that by simply trusting God—hocus pocus— out pops saints! On this view, God has undertaken all the heavy-lifting necessary to produce a holy result in human existence.

Christians happily admit there is good reason for understanding Paul's gospel in this profoundly God-centered way. After all, "to talk of the holiness of God is to summarize the being and works of the Holy Trinity,"[3] and God is in the business of transforming sinners into saints. Readers who have experienced God's transforming grace for themselves therefore expect to find in Scripture witnesses of a holy God whose grace sanctifies people for loving communion with God (see 1 Cor 6:11). And so it is that when we read through the corpus of Pauline letters, we are awestruck but not necessarily surprised to find repeated claims of the enormity of God's love in sending forth the Son to purify everyone from sin to live holy lives. Wesley rightly un-

3. Webster, *Holiness*, 77.

derstood that the sanctification of the "altogether Christian" is a work of genuine repentance grounded in trust. Real holiness is impossible without a firm faith in God's capacity to transform bad news into good news. Sanctification is a work-order that only God can fill. Paul seems to imply as much when writing to the church in Corinth, whose pews seemed filled with all kinds of spiritually immature ("carnal") members; yet, he still greets them as "sanctified in Christ Jesus" (1 Cor 1:2)?! Doesn't this suggest that Christians are holy not because they live holy lives but because God declares them so—a legal but not a real holiness? If God's sovereignty over creation is exercised by divine edict, surely such declarations of who are holy (those in Christ) and who are not (those outside of Christ) are not only legit but the manner by which God takes control of caring for the world!

But Wesley is also alert to the dangers of *sola fideism* according to which sanctification by grace through faith alone means that covenant-keeping requires nothing from us. God's grace is cooperant, not coercive grace. While our faith in God's faithfulness in effect invites God to work salvation out in our lives and relationships, the holy life is formed in the believer as the fruit of hardworking repentance. The reborn believer's cooperation with God is active, responsive, disciplined, worshipful and persistently faithful. Again, faith (by which we gain God's favor) and the fruit of genuine repentance (by which we retain God's favor) are necessary responses to God's grace whereby God's full salvation is worked out within saints.[4]

In his canonical but neglected sermon "The Nature of Enthusiasm," Wesley poses the question, "But how shall I know

---

4. This is why God's covenant-initiating grace is distributed through covenant relationships. The spiritual formation of individual believers needs to be located within the worshiping community because God's Spirit resides there; the believer's re-formation into God's likeness cannot be detached from the formative practices of the worshiping community to which she belongs. While God's saving grace transforms the believer from embodying bad news into good news, the church is custodian of the means of God's sanctifying grace.

what is the will of God in such and such a particular case?"[5] His appeal to Scripture to find an answer is typically Protestant. But what he finds there is not the analogy of faith that constrains our search for God's will in Scripture. Instead Wesley finds a "general rule" which attends to the effect of our understanding and application of God's will: "It is [God's] will that we should be inwardly and outwardly holy, that we should *be good and do good* in every kind, and in the highest degree whereof we are capable."[6] Simply put, the anticipated result of interpreting Scripture in agreement with God's purpose is a holy life.

Perhaps for this reason, in his sermons Wesley constantly interpreted Scripture's Pauline witness alongside the collective witness of the Jerusalem "Pillars," namely James, Peter, and John. In this apostolic deposit of seven letters known today as the "Catholic Epistles," the practice and product of a holy life are explored more persistently than in the Pauline witness. The interactivity of both collections of letters, Pauline (Romans–Philemon) and Pillars (James–Jude), whether to correct or to bring balance to our use of the other, helps the Spirit form a church that is fully aware of a biblical understanding of Christian discipleship. Think of it in the way the Letter of James expresses it: faith (the Pauline witness) is made complete by works (the Pillars witness) (see Jas 2:22). Both collections of New Testament letters are necessary to get a "complete" sense of discipleship and avoid the distortions that sometimes come when a congregation uses only Romans or perhaps only James to fashion its spiritual wisdom. For the most part, Protestants are weaned on the milk of Pauline teaching and assume a Pauline definition of holiness as normative—as both necessary and sufficient. If so, then a life of holiness is the effect of God's grace received by faith. They may even suppose their sainthood is simply a legal standing before God that God grants as unmerited favor: Holiness is not necessarily something they

5. "The Nature of Enthusiasm," 54.
6. Ibid., 54–55.

47

are or do but a standing of sainthood they receive and God only knows.

Embodying Godly Holiness

But the addition of a lived holiness emphasized in the Pillars collection gets us closer to the whole truth of the matter: Since God's grace has purified our hearts, transforming us into "new creatures," and since God has given us the indwelling Spirit who is holy, disciples of the living Christ are now able to embody God's holiness in their moral and spiritual practices. From the perspective of the New Testament when taken as a whole witness to God's gospel, if the certain sound of Paul's letters interprets holiness as the singular effect of divine action upon the church, its complement witness in the collection of the Catholic Epistles exhorts this same community to respond actively in holy ways. In other words, the biblical witness to the holy life is more full than an accounting of God's purifying grace upon the sinful heart through faith in Christ alone; it includes a description of the holy life that exchanges those impure practices that might contaminate fellowship with God and one another for those virtues that engage the world with works of mercy and justice.

Strikingly, the Greek word for "purify" (*hagnizo*), well known to readers of the Greek Old Testament, is not found in the Pauline canon. But in three different Catholic Epistles, this word is used at strategic moments to define actions believers must take to purify themselves in order to maintain their holy communion with God. In fact, each use is in an instruction addressed to believers as part of a longer passage that examines the character of Christian existence. Consider the following passages: James 4:8 ("Draw near to God, sinners, make pure your hearts"), 1 Peter 1:22 ("You have purified your souls by obeying the truth"), and finally and most dramatically, 1 John 3:3 ("Every person who hopes in [Jesus] purifies himself even as [Jesus] is pure") (author's translations).

Several features of this triad of verses are noteworthy. (1) Unlike the note sounded by Paul that sanctification is God's gracious work upon believers, the verbal aspect in each of these three texts is active: Believers *actively* respond in obedience to a holy God. (2) While the first two texts address the entire community, the final verse addresses the individual believer who places her hope in Christ's victory over sin for all to see. In fact, 1 John 3:3 adds the singular pronoun *eautou* ("himself") to create a reflexive sense: the individual believer takes purity upon herself to perform. And this rite of purification is not less than to cease sinning in imitation of God's Son, Jesus, in whose faithful purity she places her hope for eternal life with God (see 1 John 3:4–10). (3) Additionally, the passage from James depicts the start of a journey to a holy place, when pilgrims cleanse themselves of profane and dirty things that may intrude or interfere with their steady pilgrimage toward God. These practices that purify believers for their rendezvous with God are not performed by God upon or within the pilgrim; they are the actions required of the pilgrim in preparation for meeting with a holy God. (4) This same dynamic is envisaged in the passage from First Peter, which predicates the loving solidarity of believers, wonderfully pictured as a community of pure hearts, on their prior obedience to the gospel message.

Read within its canonical setting, the witness of these Catholic Epistles complements the prior Pauline witness by stipulating that a faithful people's holy works is the condition that forms *koinonia* or fellowship with the triune God. The community's performance of good works, quite apart from but still integral to faith, is the *mutual* effect of God's sanctifying grace at work in a people who freely respond by living a holy life in a manner that heralds the coming victory of God. On that day, Second Peter promises that a life of holiness will feel right at home because it will be set within the bounds of a new creation (2 Pet 3:11–13).

6

Practicing Holiness

Advice from First Peter

Robert R. Drovdahl

"BAD COMPANY CORRUPTS GOOD character." This ancient proverb reminds us that the company we keep can shape our character and reputation. This truth may explain why parents are so interested in their children's friends.

The proverb's truth is primarily about the world of relationships, but we can also think about its truth in other "worlds." In the world of language, for example, the same truth can be applied to words and their "character." Words acquire reputations based on the company they keep. We call a word's reputation its "connotation." A word's connotation is determined by its associations. When a word gets associated with distasteful ideas or actions, it develops a negative connotation. What connotation does *holiness* have for you? Before beginning our study of holiness, let us acknowledge the simple reality that for many, the word "holiness" feels like a corrupted term. It has unfortunately kept company with some shady characters: "dos and don'ts" legalism; "holier than thou" judgmentalism; and "holy war" fanaticism. For many, holiness does not top their lists of desirable character qualities.

Contemporary media have not helped since they often portray "holy" people negatively. Will Gluck's 2010 comedy *Easy A* provides a typical example. The Sony Pictures' film retells Nathaniel Hawthorne's classic story *The Scarlet Letter* in a contemporary context (a high school in Southern California). Emma Stone plays Olive Penderghast, a little-noticed high school student whose best friend, Rhiannon, invites her to go on a camping trip with her family. Olive doesn't want to go, so she lies to Rhiannon by telling her she has a date with a college freshman that weekend. When asked by Rhiannon on Monday about the date, Olive extends the lie by saying she had sex with the boy. Olive's story is overheard by Marianne, leader of a very visible band of Christians at the school. Thanks to Marianne, rumors fly and soon Olive's reputation is corrupted. Olive's corruption, however, is ironic in two ways. First, it is not true. Second, Olive uses her newfound negative reputation to help her friends improve their reputations. From the film's perspective, Olive is the admirable hero, the "bad" girl who does "good." From the film's perspective the truly corrupted characters are Marianne and her friends.

Marianne and her friends parallel the New England townspeople in *The Scarlet Letter*. Marianne's dad pastors a local church, and she leads small group prayer meetings on the campus. She evangelizes and is an outspoken advocate for pure living. Like the townspeople in the novel, Marianne heaps scorn and contempt upon Olive. Marianne is supposedly "holy," but she behaves quite corruptly. She is judgmental (she proclaims a higher power will judge Olive for her indecency), condescending (she sourly tells Olive that she hopes Olive used protection), and self-righteous. It's clearly the "good" characters who are really the antagonists in the film.

Such is the typical portrayal of holy people and holy living. It is not a pretty picture! Who wants to be like Marianne and her friends? Who would want to be called holy? Yet this is exactly what God wants Christians to be—holy! Nowhere is this more clearly presented than in the New Testament letter of First Peter.

Listen to Peter's command to exiled Christians: "be holy your-selves in all your conduct; for it is written, 'You shall be holy, for I am holy'" (1 Pet 1:15–16).

This chapter examines First Peter's teaching on holiness. By studying Peter's positive picture of holy living, we gain insight for practicing holiness in ways that create positive associations for holy living. After we examine four themes in Peter's perspective on holiness, we will then examine Peter's counsel for practicing holiness.

Peter's Perspective on Holiness

In contrast to contemporary portrayals of holiness as rules-oriented legalism, rigid fanaticism, or self-righteous judgmental-ism, Peter presents a compelling picture of holy people and holy living. Let's consider four themes in Peter's portrayal of holiness.

Holiness is a Desirable Quality

Three times in the letter's five chapters, Peter lifts up holiness as a desirable goal of Christian living. As God's people, we are called to a life of holiness by none other than the God who chose us for salvation (1:2, 15). Christians are described as holy priests and a holy nation, chosen by God to offer spiritual sacrifices and pro-claim God's mighty acts (2:5, 9). Peter commends holy women in times past for their conduct (3:5), and holiness is central to Peter's vision for exiled Christians growing into salvation (2:2).

Peter clearly wants holiness to characterize our conduct. We are to be holy in all our conduct (1:15). Holiness will produce honorable conduct among non-believers (2:12). A wife's conduct may be instrumental in winning an unbelieving husband to the faith (3:1). We are to exhibit "good conduct in Christ" even when we are wrongly maligned (3:16). The Greek word Peter uses for conduct is *anastrophe*. It means more than a single behavior or action. The prefix *ana* adds the idea of "through" to *strophe*, meaning "behavior"; thus, *anastrophe* implies conduct "in motion." "Manner of life" or "way of life" best convey this meaning. Authentic holiness cannot be reduced to a set of rigid rules.

Holiness is Both Active and Receptive

For Peter, practicing holiness as a way of life has a *receptive* (being) side and an *active* (doing) side. The receptive side has priority. When Peter explains how Christians grow into salvation, the first move is receiving from Jesus. Just as Jesus was chosen and precious in God's sight, so Christians, as living stones, are also chosen and precious in God's sight. We are to "let [ourselves] be built into a spiritual house, to be a holy priesthood" (2:5). The verb Peter uses in this verse is technically called an indicative, passive verb. The verb's *indicative* form suggests this project is not wishful thinking but in fact what God is doing. Holiness is not an unattainable goal, but a reality God wants to create in us. The verb's *passive* form emphasizes that God causes the action. God builds us into a spiritual house and holy priesthood. This leaves no room in authentic holiness for a judgmentalism that suggests "I am better than you." If we want to practice holiness, we might begin each day reminding ourselves, "I am precious and chosen by God to be a holy priest. I want to live my identity today."

Once we firmly ground our identity in the receptive side of holiness, we can practice the active side of holiness. Holy priests have work to do! Notice Peter's shift from the facts about how life *is* to commands about how life *should be*: "Conduct yourselves honorable among the Gentiles" (2:12). In the next three paragraphs (2:13—3:8), Peter addresses very specific conduct for first century Christians in the roles of citizen, slave, and spouse. Honorable conduct *among the Gentiles* includes obeying commands to honor the emperor (2:17), accepting the authority of one's master (2:18), adorning oneself modestly (3:3), and show-ing consideration to one's wife (3:7).

Holiness is Context Dependent

Holy conduct for Peter's first readers included praying for the emperor, not wearing braided hair, and accepting the authority of slave owners. Does holy conduct require the same behavior from twenty-first century Christians? Is braiding my hair really unholy conduct? Shouldn't we seek to end slavery rather than accept it? The third theme in Peter's letter shows that holy living may be more complicated than we might think.

When he gives specific commands for holy behavior, Pe-ter always has a purpose and context in mind. This awareness is most readily apparent in the section from 2:11—3:7. Behind the specific practices Peter commands of Christians as citizens, slaves, and spouses is a strategic purpose: "for the Lord's sake" (2:13). Peter wants his readers to conduct themselves in ways that Gentiles might see as honoring God. When we make con-textual practices into universal principles, we risk turning spe-cific holiness practices for a given time and place into a rigid set of rules for all times and places. This tendency is precisely why holiness has acquired a bad reputation for some people. The Christian community's task is to ask afresh, "In our context, how should holiness be practiced?" This question follows precisely Peter's counsel to his first readers: "Conduct yourselves honor-ably among the Gentiles" (2:12). It also echoes Jesus' instruction to his disciples in the Sermon on the Mount: "Let your light shine before others, so that they may see your good works and give glory to your Father in heaven" (Matt 5:16). We need to ask anew in our time and place, "What actions will be perceived by those around us as honoring God?"

Holiness is an Attribute and an Attitude

Peter's fourth theme is that holy living includes *doing holy things/ avoiding unholy things* and *making life holy.* Holiness is both a characteristic of behaviors and an attitude people bring to behaviors. On the attribute side of holiness, Peter wants his readers to exchange unholy living for holy living. Peter reminds his readers they were ransomed from their futile conduct by the blood of Christ (1:18–19). This futile way of life has been exchanged for honorable conduct that glorifies God. The theme of exchange runs throughout the letter. Peter wants Christians to rid themselves of ways of life that are really ways of death (see his lists in 2:1, 3:10–11, and 4:3), exchanging these ways of death for a truly blessed life. This exchange is not a grit-your-teeth, grind-it-out, miserable way of life but rather a means of achieving what we want most in life—the opportunity to live out our identity as God's holy priests.

We need to ask, "Am I engaging in any conduct that is futile and destructive to God's purposes for my life?" Peter spells out a long list of futile and destructive behaviors Christians need to clean out of their lives: malice, guile, insincerity, envy, slander, licentiousness, passions, drunkenness, revels, carousing, and lawless idolatry.

While this dimension of holiness is important, it is not the entire picture of holy living. The second way of being holy in all our conduct is making all of life holy. Holy conduct is more than labeling some activities holy (such as worshiping with the body of believers, serving the poor, reading Scripture, or praying) and labeling other activities unholy (you can make the list!). Holy conduct is an attitude we bring to all of life's activities. By our attitude we can hallow all of life. To "hallow" something means to "make holy" or to "consecrate." In this sense we can take activities that are not holy and make them holy. As we learn to hallow all of life we grow into salvation (2:2) and become holy in all our conduct.

To illustrate why both sides of holiness are essential, imagine a college student's life at a Christian college or university. If holiness is only a matter of avoiding unholy activities and engaging in some holy activities, a student's experience could easily collapse into a "dos and don'ts" form of holiness: do go to chapel; don't cheat on exams; do join a small group Bible study, don't get drunk. This limited understanding would not help a student know how to hallow studying biology, playing intramural volleyball, participating in the residence hall talent show, or working at a part-time job at the coffee shop. Holy wholeness will learn how to make everything holy.

How does this process of hallowing all our conduct work? Peter claims this comes from drinking pure, spiritual milk (2:2). The phrase "spiritual milk" is best understood as a metaphor. As a newborn needs milk to grow physically, young Christians need spiritual milk to grow spiritually. According to Peter, as we take in spiritual milk we are built up so that we can offer spiritual sacrifices to God (2:5). For Peter, disciplined love is the spiritual milk we need to hallow all of life.

Practicing Holiness through Disciplined Love

Peter wants Christians to "have genuine mutual love [and to] love one another deeply from the heart" (1:22). Holiness is practicing a way of life that places love front and center in our relationships. In 4:1–9, Peter issues numerous commands to follow yet concludes with: "*Above all* (italics added), maintain constant love for one another, for love covers a multitude of sins" (4:8). Practicing holiness means practicing love of neighbor.

If above all we are to practice love, we need self-discipline. Peter repeatedly calls his readers to this need. Peter reminds them who they are in Christ and then commands them to become who they are in Christ through self-discipline. In 1:13, Peter commands his readers to prepare their minds for action and to discipline themselves.

What does disciplined love look like in action? We conclude this study by examining a brief section of Peter's letter (4:1–9) for an answer to this question. Peter opens this section by reminding his audience that they have died to their past life. They had lived long enough in the lifestyle of the Gentiles; they needed to exchange living by their human desires for living by the will of God (4:1–6). This exchange does not happen magically in a moment. It comes from serious and self-disciplined actions in light of God's impending judgment (4:7). Four actions are commended by Peter: prayer, constant love, hospitality, and service.

The disciplines of prayer, constant love, hospitality, and service are less about avoiding the unholy or practicing the holy than about hallowing everyday life. Suppose we woke up each day with a plan to live a holy life by hallowing as much of the day's activities as possible. Let's look at these four practices in the course of a day.

Prayer

If we disciplined ourselves for the sake of our prayers (4:7), we would surely begin the day with prayer. Our beginning prayer might ask God to make us alert to where God can be found in our world and how we might participate in God's purposes throughout our day. We would then seek to practice a prayerful attitude throughout the day, aiming to keep Paul's command to pray without ceasing (1 Thess 5:17). A classic form of practicing prayerfulness is repeating often the Jesus Prayer, "Lord Jesus Christ, Son of God, have mercy on me, a sinner." Our repeated prayer might be, "Lord Jesus Christ, Son of God, open my eyes to your presence today." This prayer can set the tone for seeing where love is most needed.

Constant Love

Prayer is the starting point for hallowing our day, but constant love is the destination. We pray so that we might better love. We need self-discipline to maintain *constant* love. Peter knows exactly when it is most difficult to practice constant love—when people fail us. They don't do what they promised. They say things that hurt us. They don't give us what we think we need from them. They let us down. They are too busy to give us the attention we want. In the face of these failings, we maintain constant love when we generously overlook these shortcomings.

Peter uses a loosely translated Old Testament proverb, "Love covers all offenses" (Prov 10:12), to suggest why *constant* love takes discipline. As human beings, we find it reasonably easy to love the lovely and the loving. Jesus told his disciples even tax collectors love those who love them (Matt 5:46). But if we are sinned against, we are not being loved and so naturally not inclined to love back. It takes discipline to practice *constant* love in the face of slights, mistreatments, and hurts we bear at the hands of others. Just as Jesus called his followers to God's higher standard of loving those who don't love us (Matt 5:43–48), Peter calls us to the higher standard of constant love, one involving the overlooking of faults we so easily notice in those around us.

Hospitality

The third practice Peter mentions, hospitality, also flows from disciplined love. If overlooking people's failings is love's response to negative interactions with others, hospitality is disciplined love's positive interaction with others. Hospitality befriends others by making room in our lives for those we engage daily. Think of all the social spaces a college student inhabits. These might include the residence halls, classrooms, labs, dining halls, and places of employment. How can we befriend others within these spaces? One strategy could include sitting next to someone one doesn't know in a class and introducing oneself. Another could be inviting that person down the hall for a late night trip to the coffee shop. We might also seek to practice intellectual hospitality. When we hear people support a political position we find disagreeable, we can learn about how they came to their position and what evidence they found most compelling. When we find an author's writing dense and difficult, we can make room to read it a second or even a third time.

Service

The fourth command Peter gives in 4:7–11 is to use our gifts to serve one another. This command blends beautifully the receptive and active sides of holiness mentioned earlier. We do not serve out of our own strength. Peter reminds his readers that the power source of service is God. We receive a gift from the manifold grace of God and we steward that gift with the strength that God supplies (4:11). Since we steward God's gracious gift, we are protected from seeing service as "doing everything anyone asks of us." Being accountable to God protects us from being at the mercy of too many immediate needs, all clamoring for our time and resources. Part of stewarding God's gifts for service is preparing to use effectively these gifts. We should prayerfully ask God to open our eyes to the service God wishes us to render throughout the day. That will help us find the balance between the immediate needs and demands that press upon us and the possibility and rise of future needs. In that balance we understand all our lives as aimed at serving others.

Peter's letter offers a healthy perspective on holiness and helpful advice for practicing holiness. Hopefully, it makes us want to keep company with holiness and make it our friend. If so, we can begin each day with a reminder that we are precious in God's sight and have been chosen by God to be holy priests. We can ask God to strengthen us to offer creative sacrifices of love for our neighbors. Then we will be alert and watchful for those opportunities. They will come because God wants us to be holy, even as God is holy.

7

A Heritage of Holiness

*Themes of Sanctification in
the Christian Tradition*

Douglas M. Strong

THROUGHOUT THE HISTORY OF the church, Christians have sought to be holy, longing for and expecting purity of heart. When pondering Jesus' admonition that we are to be "perfect, just as [our] Father in heaven is perfect" (Matt 5:48), believers over the centuries have held the conviction that God actually wanted them to be like Christ in this life and not trapped in an unrelenting cycle of sinful actions. Christians, therefore, have boldly prayed that God will produce holiness in them—not only some day in heaven, but even right now.

Holiness has been a central theme of Christian spirituality throughout the Christian tradition. It is an especially common motif in the devotional resources of the Christian heritage. Over the years, the great majority of Christian theologians have insisted that God provides the opportunity for believers to be pure of heart, though such theologians have differed in how they conceived this purity coming about. Their differences were manifested in various questions they asked, such as: Is holiness a gift of grace or the product of (or reward for) pious effort? Can it be realized in this life? Can people be considered "saints" even if they are merely on the way toward holiness and have not yet attained it? Over the duration of the church's history, Christian writers did not talk about holiness uniformly; therefore, the long tradition of Christianity has approached the topic with variety—and sometimes even ambiguity.

The Early and Pre-Modern Church

Many of the ancient "fathers" of the church spoke about God's call to sanctification. Indeed, most of the earliest Christians assumed that holy living was not only possible but necessary for baptized Christians. The common understanding in the church was that the sacrament of baptism cleansed believers thoroughly from all sin; thereafter, the Christian should be living a life of perfect love toward God and neighbor. It is understandable, then, that a central pastoral problem for the early church was how to deal with a person's sin after baptism. But most ancient Christians also understood that holiness grew gradually in a person and that "perfection" was relative and not absolute.

In the second century, Irenaeus of Lyons addressed these issues by affirming that all believers in Christ are in the process of being "deified"—becoming increasingly like God through the agency of the Holy Spirit. He stated at one point, "[Christ became] what we are, that he might bring us to be even what he is himself."[1] God sent Christ to become a person—to suffer, die and be resurrected—for the purpose of recreating us in God's image. Jesus Christ has already instituted a new creation, and we are invited to be participants in that holy endeavor. "Little by little, we are being conditioned to receive and bear God."[2] Our sanctification—being set apart by God for a holy purpose—is at

1. *Against Heresies*, Book V, preface.
2. *Against Heresies*, V, 8, 1.

the center of the divine intent for human beings. "Through the infusion of the Holy Spirit, the human being becomes spiritual and perfect. This is what brings the believer to the image and likeness of God."[3]

Another church father, Clement of Alexandria, who lived shortly after Irenaeus, described Christ as both the instructor of true knowledge and the content of that knowledge. This knowledge is given only by Christ, who reveals himself to us; through him, we truly know both God and ourselves. When one knows God, that person has been made capable of being a dwelling place of the Holy Spirit, whose presence purifies the one in whom the Spirit dwells. That person "is destined to become like God and is already being taken into God."[4] Clement saw purification as a divine gift, given to all Christians in baptism, so that they may love God and neighbor perfectly.

Gregory of Nyssa lived in the fourth century at a time of great change when the church was being legitimized and even favored by the Roman Empire. While this recognition of the church had the positive effect of ending the persecution of believers, it also tended to create the conditions for moral compromise among nominal Christians. Gregory and two other deeply thoughtful Christian leaders (the three often referred to as the "Cappadocian Fathers") became highly influential theologians by speaking into this context. They asked: How do we live out the Christian life in less than ideal circumstances? Gregory answered this important question by stating that God has given us the freedom to will rightly or wrongly. God has given us grace to be able to choose the path of holiness—following Christ as our model and receiving his resurrection power. Our aim is to be conformed to the image of Christ through the operation of the Holy Spirit, especially by exercising the means of grace offered by the church.

---

3. *Against Heresies*, V, 6, 1.
4. *Stromata*, VII, 1.

Over time, the standard expectation regarding sanctification lessened among ordinary Christians. Monks and nuns, however, continued to take the call to a holy life very seriously, for their monastic devotion aimed at a life of Christ-like perfect love. This vision was a very attractive ideal, even if it sometimes went sour or became corrupt. Monks engaged in various spiritual practices with the goal of encountering God in company with God's people. They lived out their yearning to become more like Christ through daily rounds of disciplined prayer in the context of a close community. When monks practiced Benedict's threefold rule of poverty, charity, and obedience, they were said to be "following the counsels of perfection." They understood themselves to be walking in the way of "evangelical perfection," which was a grace-given inclination to do the whole will of God, resulting from a heart filled with the love of Christ. They trusted that the Spirit could completely cleanse the heart from all that is willfully contrary to the love of God. Monastic leaders, such as Bernard of Clairvaux in the twelfth century, stressed that a holy life and its character are part of God's plan for believers in the here and now. Christians are called to love God supremely but that can come only through the removal of human pride and self-centeredness. Bernard wrote that such love is a gift of God. Mystics, too—such as Catherine of Siena and Julian of Norwich—described their deep, interior love for Christ.

One difficulty, however, with monastic practice was that only monks and nuns were viewed as "religious" by society at large; by the medieval period, all other baptized Christians—the vast majority—were not expected to be able to live a holy life. Another problematic aspect of medieval piety was the practice of designating particular (usually dead) exemplary Christians as "saints," leaving the rest of the people as everyday sinners. The hope was that average Christians would model their lives after the "great charity and heroic virtue" of the recognized saints, but in practice, most church people felt that they could never measure up and thus were resigned to a life of spiritual mediocrity and moral failure.

The Protestant Reformation

By the sixteenth century, the perceived distinction in the Western Church between beatified saints and everyone else created a situation in which a number of abuses developed in the practice of Catholic spirituality. Taking advantage of the fear of imminent death prevalent during that era, especially after the spread of the bubonic plague, some church officials exploited the commoners' worry that they or their loved ones would be consigned to hell, or at least would have to spend a long stint in purgatory as expiation for their sins. One form that this exploitation took was the promotion of indulgences—payments made to the church that were supposed to be an expression of the sinner's gratitude for God's forgiveness; in practice, however, indulgences were perceived by many people as a monetary means for lessening one's purgatory time. An additional difficulty was that the only way of receiving this forgiveness was through the ministrations of the sacramental system of the hierarchical church as regulated by the priests— some of whom had profited from the sale of indulgences.

Martin Luther's well-known critique of the late medieval Western Church was largely a reaction to these abuses. By emphasizing Paul's argument that justification is by grace through faith, Luther taught that God's favor is available freely through the action of Christ's death on our behalf without any work on our part. We are covered over with Christ's imputed righteousness, Luther taught, and we will never be able to produce righteousness in ourselves because sinfulness for Christians is inevitable. We are justified believers and sinners at the same time.

In terms of the possibility of holiness in believers, Luther became concerned that any stress on a Christian's virtuous behavior might be perceived as something which could earn salvation. Consequently, sanctification for Luther was seen simply as a natural development of justification. Sanctification was not a second element of salvation; it was nothing more than appreciating one's justification and living out its reality in one's life. Luther did not believe that we could "grow" more holy because to teach that would imply that something needed to be added to our already accomplished justification. As a result, many in the Lutheran tradition tended to neglect the concept of sanctification, implicitly negating the idea that ongoing spiritual transformation is essential to the Christian idea of salvation.

But not all outcomes of the Reformation resulted in a downgrade of the emphasis on holy living; an interesting and significant shift, for instance, occurred in the sixteenth century regarding the Protestant view of the extent of God's work among people. Does God work more particularly among those whom the church views as "religious" than among common Christians? Luther's answer to this question was an unequivocal "no." Rather, Luther affirmed that all Christians are "priests"—capable of approaching God on their own and offering divine forgiveness to one another on God's behalf. Other reformers, such as John Calvin, similarly emphasized that every believer had a Christian "vocation"—a call by God to lead a life of piety. This Protestant shift toward the equalization of the divine call on all people created theological space for the idea, among some, that all people are also given the opportunity to be made holy.

Calvin, for example, taught that God's law was a necessary rule to guide the behavior of Jesus' disciples so that every Christian could grow in sanctification. By emphasizing the essentiality of living a more holy life following one's justification, Calvin differed somewhat from Luther and helped to create a religious environment in Reformed (Calvinist) churches that stressed the importance of spiritual growth among Christians.

Thomas Cranmer, the Anglican Archbishop during this era, believed even more deeply that the medieval monastic perspective on holy living could and should be brought into the normal life of any Christian. Every believer should (1) aim at a life of perfect love, of Christlikeness, lived in the everyday human community and (2) balance labor, study, worship, and prayer. With these things in mind, Cranmer created a prayer book—one that was not just for monks but a "Book of Common Prayer." "Common" meant "for everyone," laypeople as well as clergy, and Cranmer's beautiful wording deliberately reflected the patterns and resources that had developed over the previous millennium.

The Anabaptists articulated yet another Reformation variation on these themes. Along with Luther, the Anabaptists believed that justification is by grace through faith, but they felt that Luther took that doctrine too far when he declared that a believer can never truly obey the law of God. Rather, through their reading of the Scriptures—especially the Sermon on the Mount—the Anabaptists insisted that the grace of God actually transforms believers and makes them righteous. They taught that sanctification—which they defined as obedience to Christ—is possible in this life, not just an ideal to be fulfilled in the life to come. For them, both justification and sanctification are by grace. God imparts as well as imputes righteousness to believers, transforming the life of Christians. The church, then, should be a fellowship of those who actually are holy.

Pietism and Wesleyanism

In the years following the Reformation, the Christian traditions in Europe (Catholic, Lutheran, Reformed, Anabaptist) disputed over increasingly narrow definitions of what each group considered to be right doctrine. Following a century (approximately 1550–1650) of brutal, religiously-motivated wars, there was a desire among late seventeenth century Europeans for an expression of Christian faith that tolerated various beliefs and that was based on one's experience of God and the practice of love toward others rather than on doctrinal correctness or precision. This faith expression came to be known as Pietism, as articulated by reformers such as the Lutheran pastor Philip J. Spener. In his well-known call to action entitled *Pia Desideria* ("pious hopes"), Spener emphasized that Christians and theologians demonstrate themselves by their godly faith, holy living, and love of God and neighbor rather than by subtle and abstract argumentation. In this light, Pietists introduced the language of holiness into the Lutheran tradition and also influenced many others as well. For example, Spener was a sponsor at the baptism of Nicholas Zinzendorf, who as an adult was to become the leader of the Moravian Brethren (another Pietist group) and who eventually became a significant influence on the developing spirituality of the eighteenth century evangelical preacher John Wesley.

Wesley was nourished both by the Pietist devotional stress on holy living through an affective experience of vital piety and by his native Anglican liturgical and theological perspective on holiness. From Anglicanism, for instance, Wesley drew the concept that sanctification was a gift for everyone—an early church ideal—and not simply a reward for the heroic pieties of a few designated saints. The experience of sanctification, Wesley taught, is a divine gift that fundamentally reconstitutes our relationships with God and others and opens up a moment-by-moment process of growth in grace as we practice holy living in the fruits of the Holy Spirit. From the Pietists, Wesley insisted that the awareness of this grace is felt in the depth of our hearts—experienced through an abiding sense of joy that comes from the Spirit's inner witness.

Whereas Wesley believed that holiness was possible for every Christian—unlike the monastic understanding—he nevertheless agreed with the monks that a life of holiness is not possible without the support of others. Wesley's system of mutually accountable discipleship in small groups was the hallmark of early Methodism and resulted in a dynamic movement of God's Spirit. Work with the poor, the unemployed, prisoners and exploited women and children grew out of this fellowship of holiness. Consequently, it is not surprising that people who lived as social outcasts felt particularly drawn to Methodism—people like miners, industrial laborers, and (eventually) African-American slaves, whose spirituals reflected the holiness message in lines such as: "Lord, I want to be more holy in my heart."

The Holiness Movement

Methodists in America continued Wesley's practices. As in all movements, however, it was difficult to keep the fervor and high level of their initial commitment. Some American Methodist laypeople neglected their small groups, and some Methodist preachers downplayed the Wesleyan distinctive of sanctification. In the mid-to-late nineteenth century, the coalition of those concerned about this neglect became known as the Holiness movement. One of the Holiness denominations established during this period, along with the Salvation Army and the Church of the Nazarene, was the Free Methodist Church—"free" because it emphasized the free grace offered by God to all people for the sanctification of their souls, the freedom of all people from slavery, and the fact that no one should be charged anything to attend church (the latter happening in some congregations where pews were rented or sold). The Free Methodists and other Holiness churches were at the forefront of efforts to end slavery, to give women equal rights with men, to end the deleterious effects of alcohol on women and children, and to eliminate class distinctions. They believed that God's summons to act righteously had very specific implications regarding how they lived out their daily lives in the nineteenth century context.

Holiness preachers emphasized particular aspects of Wesley's teachings on Christian perfection, such as the idea that sanctification will be manifested both in moral behavior and in a specific, profound spiritual experience. This experience of "entire sanctification" typically followed one's "new birth" experience and was therefore described as a "second blessing." Holiness people linked the "secondness" and momentary nature of sanctification with the biblical concept of the "baptism of the Holy

Spirit." Later, in the early twentieth century, Pentecostals also stressed a subsequent blessing; their understanding of "Spirit baptism" associated this experience with the reception of spiritual gifts (such as speaking in tongues) in addition to spiritual fruits (which resulted in holy living).

Concluding Remarks

This holiness heritage continued into the twentieth century when Roman Catholic social activists, such as Dorothy Day (and the Catholic Worker movement) and Gustavo Gutiérrez (and Latin American liberation theologians), began to link their pursuit for social justice with the pursuit for holiness. Their conviction that God has a preferential option for the poor led them to be convinced that when one wants to become more Christ-like, one will advocate for those on the margins of society so that the kingdom of God may be more fully realized here on earth.

In each of these eras throughout the church's history, Christians of all stripes were convinced that God would give them the power to live a holy life for the sake of God's reign. This heritage is one worth claiming and embodying even today.

8

Radical Holiness and Gender

Priscilla Pope-Levison

And here we come to the point, and are forced to an answer to which in the name of the Head of the church we claim a rejoinder. Our answer is this: The Christian churches of the present day, with but few exceptions, have imposed silence on Christian woman, so that her voice may but seldom be heard in Christian assemblies[1]

MORE THAN 150 YEARS have come and gone since Phoebe Palmer penned these words, and opportunities have both arisen and arrested for Protestant women in public ministry. In Palmer's own church, the United Methodist Church, avenues of ministry for women increased more and more throughout the opening decades of the twentieth century until every obstacle came down in 1956 when by General Conference vote women were granted full ministerial status. Women now serve at every level of the local and national church, from an ordained minister celebrating word and sacrament for a congregation to a bishop overseeing a multitude of ministers. At least for Palmer's own church, women's voices are silent no longer; they are loud and clear in United Methodist assemblies.

1. Palmer, *Promise of the Father*, 5.

However, American Protestants are by no means unanimous on this issue; in fact, opposing stances on women's roles in ministry divide believer from believer. Unlike the United Methodist Church, within conservative Protestantism, gender is *the* factor that keeps women from certain offices in the church. In other words, giftedness for ministry is subsumed by the prior question of gender. As the doctrinal statement of the Southern Baptist Convention states in the simplest of terms: "While both men and women are gifted for service in the church, the office of pastor is limited to men as qualified by Scripture."[2] In contrast to such a view, this essay will argue, following Jesus' example, that a commitment to holiness empowers Christians to forge radical ways of justice and equality with regard to gender.

Sex and Gender within Protestantism

Gender is a "powerful means of orienting world and self"—and church—because it is inextricably tied up with the social construction of what it means to be male and female.[3] Gender is often interpreted as synonymous with sex, but such a move is a misnomer. Whereas sex is a biological and physical term, gender is a social and cultural term. One learns one's gender—how to act as male or female—through instruction and observation of one's family, society, church, school, and other such institutions. The behavior associated with gender is what constitutes a "gender role." Gender roles are constructed around "organized patterns of behavior we follow that are based on our interpretation of the significance of sex."[4]

Within conservative American Protestantism, a strict construction of gender roles is at the fulcrum of heated debate. In her study of evangelical Christian women, Julie Ingersoll asserts

---

2. http://www.sbc.net/bfm/bfm2000.asp#iii. Accessed on 6 June 2011.

3. Bendroth, *Fundamentalism and Gender*, 6.

4. Sapiro, *Women in American Society*, 68.

that an unequivocal commitment to complementarian gender roles currently ranks for this generation of evangelicals as a paramount priority, as significant as the debate on biblical inerrancy was in the previous generation. Using as a case study a Southern Baptist seminary, Ingersoll demonstrates that the pivotal litmus test for potential faculty members has now shifted from a scrutiny of their stance on inerrancy to their adherence to complementarian gender roles, particularly in terms of male leadership in the church. A faculty member hired in 1992 was told by the president that his affirmative position on women in ministry would have prevented his being hired three years later. As Ingersoll explains, "Inerrancy is no longer the central issue. [This seminary] has moved from considering a candidate's views on the issue of women's ordination as only an indication of that candidate's views on inerrancy to making hiring decisions solely on the basis of a candidate's views on that issue [women as pastors]."[5]

Within conservative American Protestantism, the most popular construction of gender roles is known as complementarianism. This stance assigns certain behaviors and roles for men that are separate and different from women's, and these are designed to complement one another. Advocates explain that complementarity simultaneously encompasses equality and difference between the genders, equality in terms of "a correspondence between man and woman" and difference in terms of roles. Woman's role is to submit to man as his helper; man's role is to lead the woman. "Woman complements man in a way that makes her a helper to him. Her role is not identical to his. Their complementarity allows them to be a partnership in which each needs the other, because each provides something different from what the other provides."[6] For some complementarians, gender roles remain in place even beyond family and church; in other words, woman must submit to man as his helper in every context. As

5. Ingersoll, *Evangelical Christian Women*, 53.
6. Clark, *Man and Woman in Christ*, 23.

a pastor of a large, Los Angeles church explains, "I would say that . . . there really shouldn't be a different structure for women in society [than there is] in the church. They would need to submit to men in general." When asked whether a female principal would ever be hired for the school housed at his church, he responded negatively because in that situation, "There would be male teachers who would then be required to submit to female leadership, which we believe would be outside the standard of God." Even single women need to be "in the context of submitting [themselves] to men in general."[7]

Complementarians find an explication of God's design for gender roles from the opening chapters of Genesis. First, they look to Genesis 1 for the declaration of equality between the genders—God created male and female in God's image (Gen 1:26–27) and assigned them jointly to take charge of the earth, to steward it together (Gen 1:28–29). Curiously, one recent commentator demarcates a gendered division of labor even in God's stewardship command in the first chapter of Genesis, a division that "assigns to the man the primary responsibility to provide for his wife and children and to the woman the care for and nurture of her family."[8] Unfortunately, this author offers no biblical citation or rationale for this claim. Then in Genesis 2, complementarians locate gender differentiation and concomitant gender roles circumscribed in several places, such as the order of God's creation of the sexes (man first and then woman) (Gen 2:7, 21–23), the prior commands God gave just to the man (Gen 2:16–17), the man's naming of the animals (Gen 2:19–20), and the creation of woman to be "a helper" (Gen 2:18). These aspects of Genesis 2 corroborate complementarians' insistence on male leadership and female submission. By rooting gender differences and hierarchical roles before the fall in Genesis 3, complementarians contend that such was God's design from the beginning of creation.

7. Ingersoll, *Evangelical Christian Women*, 17–18.
8. Köstenberger, *God, Marriage, and Family*, 24.

A complementarian worldview regulates every aspect of life, from romance and marriage to career aspirations and parenting. In recent studies of female college students, investigators trace the comparison between a complementarian and an egalitarian worldview on their future plans. Females in the complementarian group were "more likely to aspire to motherhood and full-time homemaker status." They also exhibited extremely high agreement with certain statements and ways of speaking, such as "The husband is the head of the home" (75.4%), "There will be limitations on what position I can hold in the church because of my gender" (88.6%), and the notion of "helper-wife" (96.7%).[9] According to Donna Freitas's findings, women in the complementarian group assume the more passive role in romance and dating as compared to their male counterparts:

> While evangelical women grow up learning the values of patience and passivity, evangelical men are raised to believe they are *active* when it comes to sex, purity, and romance: they *guard* their women, they *prove* themselves chivalrous by heroic restraint, they *take* a woman's gift [of virginity] as their birthright. Women by contrast, *submit* to their guardian, and they *wait* for their prince to come along and for their purity to *be taken* on their wedding day.[10]

To solidify their position against what they perceive as an encroaching egalitarianism in the home, church, and society, complementarians assume an embattled pose, an "us versus them" stance. The first to come under attack are feminists, followed closely by any woman who does not conform to their prescribed gender roles. A galvanizing document for complementarians, the 1987 Danvers Statement of The Council for Biblical Manhood and Womanhood, focuses on two culprits for the current contention surrounding the complementarian outlook: feminists—"the increasing promotion given to feminist

9. Tangenberg, "Women's Mentoring on Christian Campuses."
10. Freitas, *Sex and the Soul*, 92.

egalitarianism"—and women who move beyond complementarian roles—"the widespread ambivalence regarding the values of motherhood, vocational homemaking, and the many ministries historically performed by women." Evidently, no corresponding confusion exists concerning men's roles in fatherhood, vocational work in the home, or the ministries men historically perform because none are mentioned in the document; in short, men never appear to be the problem, only women. In a concluding dire prediction, the Danvers statement portends, "We are convinced that a denial or neglect of these principles will lead to increasingly destructive consequences in our families, our churches, and the culture at large."[11]

The Example of Jesus Christ

In contrast to a complementarian construction of gender roles, which assigns male and female to predetermined, fixed roles from conception, this essay contends that a full-orbed commitment to holiness liberates believers to pursue a radical love of God and neighbor. The horizontal dimension of such a love emanates from its vertical axis—love for and loyalty to God—and it is not classified or choreographed by distinctions like gender, race, and class. "Holiness is more than a proposition; it is a passion. It is more than loyalty to a doctrine; it is loyalty to a Person. It is not merely a creed; it is a life. To be a Christian is to be a true lover of Jesus Christ. . . . When we know Him in this way He becomes the supreme object of our love."[12] Therefore, the radical features of holiness compel believers to love Jesus Christ and to love those whom he loves.

If we turn again to the issue of gender, it is clear that Jesus' treatment of women exhibits a divergent trajectory from the patriarchal, oppressive culture of his day. He approaches women

11. "Danvers Statement," 471.

12. Vennard, "Friendship with Christ," 3.

with compassion, friendship, even equality; as Elizabeth Johnson explains, "Through his ministry Jesus unleashes a hope, a vision, and a present experience of liberating relationships that women, the lowest of the low in any class, as well as men, savor as the antithesis of patriarchy. Women interact with Jesus in mutual respect, support, comfort, and challenge."[13] Instances of these liberating relationships between Jesus and women abound in the Gospels, such as his conversation with the Samaritan woman (the longest between Jesus and another person); his acceptance of and compassion toward the woman who dared to break into an all-male dinner party and anoint his feet with her tears; his mature friendships with Mary and Martha; his appearance in risen form to Mary Magdalene and his charge to her (one who was not a male disciple) to proclaim the news of his resurrection.

However, among the trajectory of liberating relationships between Jesus and women, the story of Jesus and the Gentile woman in Matthew 15:21–28 seems to be an exception. At first, Jesus doesn't even bother to answer her, even though she shouts at him in such a way that his disciples can hear her raucous exclamations. Only when his disciples implore him to send her away does Jesus acknowledge her with a curt response, which seems intended to silence her and send her on her way. Rather than being silenced, however, she engages Jesus in an interchange, one that completely alters what appears to be Jesus' intention *not* to grant her request that he heal her daughter. "[Jesus] answered, 'I was sent only to the lost sheep of the house of Israel.' But she came and knelt before him, saying, 'Lord, help me.' He answered, 'It is not fair to take the children's food and throw it to the dogs.' She said, 'Yes, Lord, yet even the dogs eat the crumbs that fall from their masters' table'" (Matt 15:24–27). The story ends not only with his compliance with her request but also with a commendation of her faith: "Then Jesus answered her, 'Woman, great is your faith! Let it be done for you as you wish.' And her daughter was healed instantly" (Matt 15:28).

13. Johnson, *She Who Is*, 157.

This christological portrait is not an elevated one in which Jesus knows beforehand and thus anticipates everything. Rather this portrait of Jesus that emerges in his encounter with the Gentile woman admits of Jesus' intimate involvement with his own humanity, such that he grows and changes in response to those around him. Even more, the recognition that Jesus learned from and dignified women, such as the Canaanite woman, empowers equality between men and women. Equality, mutuality, men and women forming friendships in the gospel's transforming power—such are the characteristics of a radical holiness which conforms to the vision of God's reign as modeled by Jesus. As Elizabeth Johnson writes, "New possibilities of relationships patterned according to the mutual services of friendship rather than domination-subordination flower among the women and men who respond and join [Jesus'] circle. They form a community of the discipleship of equals."[14] This vision of Jesus' community, which anticipates the inclusiveness of God's reign, should inspire the church today to pattern its ministry after such a mutuality between men and women, old and young, leader and laity.

A Protestant Alternative from History

Such beliefs about women's full and equal participation in the church can be traced back within Protestantism more than four hundred years to the emergence of the Quaker movement of the seventeenth century. From the outset, the Quakers attested to the full equality of men and women in the family, church, and society. This belief was grounded in the Bible, according to Margaret Fell's 1666 pamphlet titled *Women's Speaking, Justified, Proved and Allowed by the Scriptures.*[15]

Recalling the example from the first part of this chapter, we note that Palmer connected holiness, power, and women's

14. Johnson, *She Who Is*, 157–8.

15. One can access this pamphlet in Thomas D. Hamm, ed., *Quaker Writings*, 95–105.

preaching. She believed that the fulfillment of Jesus' promise in Luke 24:49, one in which believers would be clothed with power from on high, occurred in the Holy Spirit's descent in "tongues of fire" at Pentecost in Acts 2. This "endowment of power" fell on both men and women: "This is what was spoken through the prophet Joel: 'In the last days it will be, God declares, that I will pour out my Spirit upon all flesh, and your sons and your daughters shall prophesy, and your young men shall see visions, and your old men shall dream dreams. Even upon my slaves, both men and women, in those days I will pour out my Spirit; and they shall prophesy'" (Acts 2:16–18). Palmer considered this the paradigmatic passage to support women preachers because it encapsulates the *promise of the Father* who has imparted to women, in the last days of this present age, the power to bear witness to the saving and sanctifying gospel of Jesus Christ. In other words, the power of the Holy Spirit, given at Pentecost, was not restricted to the New Testament era; according to Palmer, it is even now available to all Christians through the experience of holiness or entire sanctification.

This experience, as interpreted by Palmer and others in the Methodist holiness movement, had two practical effects. First, through the empowerment of women, there would be many more people available to preach the gospel than if preaching were restricted to men. The church, then, would have at its disposal the personnel for bringing "tens of thousands more" to conversion. Second, holiness imparted to women a "holy boldness" for preaching, allowing them to have the power to preach like never before. One evangelist described this boldness as enabling her to overcome the man-fearing spirit in her that prevented her from preaching. Mary Lee Cagle, a minister in the Church of the Nazarene, was quite timid when she first began to preach, but she prayed that God would turn her loose, and her prayer for "holy boldness" was answered, as she explained in her autobiography:

> [God] turned her loose—absolutely broke every fetter. . . . It was the first time in her life that she could

> turn the pulpit loose—she ran from one end of the large platform to the other and shouted and praised God, and preached with the Holy Ghost sent down from above. . . . It was a permanent loosing from that day, and she has never been bound again. Although of a shrinking, backward disposition, she has never seen a crowd since that day large enough to make her knees tremble, and she has preached to thousands.[16]

Given the testimony of Acts and the Spirit's work of calling and empowering women for ministry, gender is insignificant in terms of who should preach. What, then, determines whether a man or woman is called to preach? If gender is not an issue in terms of who should preach, then what is? For B.T. Roberts, founder of the Free Methodist Church, the essential issue was whether there was evidence of God's calling on the person by an affirmative answer to three questions: Has she grace? Has she gifts? Has she fruits? As Roberts explains in his short pamphlet, *The Right of Women to Preach the Gospel*, "The claim of a woman, to be called of God to preach the Gospel, should not then, be rejected because she is a woman. Apply to her the same tests that you apply to a man. You judge whether a woman should teach a school, or edit a paper, in the same way that you judge whether a man should do these things. This is proper. Try in the same way her supposed call to preach the Gospel."[17]

This message from saints of the past presses us in the present to insist on a radical shift in those Christian communities where there still exists an assignment of positions and roles according to gender. In some of these communities, women would never be allowed to preach or speak in a public gathering; in others, a woman can only preach if there is a male authority over her as the teaching elder. This gender-based division runs counter to Paul's exhortation in Galatians 3:28: "There is no longer Jew or Greek, there is no longer slave or free, there is no longer male

---

16. Cagle, *Life and Work of Mary Lee Cagle*, 29.

17. Roberts, *The Right of Women to Preach the Gospel*, 9–10.

and female; for all of you are one in Christ Jesus." Further, as we have seen, holiness as power imparts intensity and strength to both men and women to make known to the whole world the good news of Jesus Christ in word, deed, song, witness, ministry, preaching, and personal lifestyle—in short, in every way possible.

9

Holiness and the Spiritual Disciplines

Jeffrey F. Keuss

We [have] become avid for spirituality: we long to be in
community, experiencing love and trust and joy with
others. We are fed up with being evaluated by how much
we can contribute, how much we can do. We hunger for
communion with God, something beyond the satisfac-
tion of self, the development of *me*. We are fed up with
being told *about* God.[1]

"You Become Responsible, Forever, for What You Have Tamed"

IN ANTOINE DE SAINT-EXUPÉRY'S wonderful 1943 children's
book *The Little Prince*, an aviator crash-lands in the middle of the
Saharan desert, and after a time of being stranded, he is awakened by a little prince who requests, "If you please—draw me
a sheep!"[2] The aviator could not draw well because grown-ups
had discouraged him to pursue painting when he was a child,

1. Peterson, *Subversive Spirituality*, 36.
2. *The Little Prince*, 9.

and yet the real matter pressing the aviator's mind is where this little boy came from. The prince didn't care at this point to answer his questions or to excuse the aviator from the task; rather than allowing the aviator to pass, the little prince remarks, "That [you cannot draw well] doesn't matter. Draw me a sheep."[3] After several failed attempts, the aviator draws a box and says that the sheep is inside, a notion that delights the little prince. It turns out, the aviator and the little prince would become friends, with the latter being quite inquisitive and, as it so happens, from another planet. The book largely documents the little prince's growing understanding of how our world functions, including some of its more bizarre features.

One very remarkable exchange takes place between the little prince and a fox that he comes to know as he is exploring earth. After some introductions, the little prince asks the fox to come play with him. The fox replies, "I cannot play with you . . . I am not tamed."[4] The little prince doesn't understand this notion of taming and persistently asks the fox what it means; the fox finally replies, "It is an act too often neglected"; he goes on to say, "It means to establish ties."[5] The little prince asks what this phrase means, to establish ties, and the fox replies, "Just that. To me, you are still nothing more than a little boy who is just like a hundred thousand other little boys. And I have no need of you. And you, on your part, have no need of me. To you, I am nothing more than a fox like a hundred thousand other foxes. But if you tame me, then we shall need each other. To me, you will be unique in all the world. To you, I shall be unique in all the world."[6] And so the little prince tames the fox, and they become good friends, but after a while, the little prince has to leave, which occasions the fox sharing some exceedingly deep remarks. First, he tells the prince a very simple secret: "It is only with the heart that one can

3. Ibid., 10.
4. Ibid.., 65.
5. Ibid., 66.
6. Ibid..

see rightly; what is essential is invisible to the eye."[7] And second, the fox claims, "Men have forgotten this truth. . . . But you must not forget it. You become responsible, forever, for what you have tamed."[8]

Taming is such an interesting notion. For some it will evoke negative connotations to be sure and in some regards it is a word that has been misused over the centuries. The tension surrounding what it means to be human is ultimately bound up in this notion of whether we are to be tamed or allowed "to go native," if you will. From the Age of Reason onward, this tension is framed by a longing to recover that which has been lost as Western culture has moved further into a technological dependence. While there was an eighteenth century longing for a seemingly simpler age, as Western culture entered the twentieth century, the desire was to be more than merely civilized, as seen in Friedrich Nietzsche's call to humanity to embrace the *Übermensch* (Superman/Over-man). In his 1896 masterwork *Thus Spoke Zarathustra*, Nietzsche sees the role of the *Übermensch* as merely our destiny: All things seek to transcend their natural state, and so humanity is destined to leave behind the Victorian age and embrace the twentieth century. Because of this heritage, Western culture has become deeply suspicious of taming. If you are a naturalist, taming evokes snuffing out the carnality and majesty out of something: powerful elephants reduced to mundane circus tricks, horses that once ran free now walking in slow circles at children's petting zoos, dogs shackled to leashes and trotted around paved sidewalks while suburbanites yak away on cell phones.

If we recall *The Little Prince*, however, taming in that book is something of another order than what Nietzsche is fixated on, and as we shall see, perhaps another word must now be employed. *In its truest sense, taming is making a tie to something; it is a tether or a bond.* It is a way to give boundary to our lives so that we do not merely walk away from our commitments but instead

7. Ibid.., 70.
8. Ibid., 71.

choose to stay put, be present, and ultimately love. Taming is not taking the divine spark out of something but rather the release of the imagination to go beyond what can be seen with the naked eye. *To tame and be tamed are not bad things.* They represent a commitment to being with each other rather than being wild for the sake of ourselves.

As you have recognized throughout your reading of this book, holiness is a form of taming. Holiness too is a call to make a deep and abiding bond with God that will permeate all aspects of our lives. In the Christian life, it is through holiness that we journey into a relationship with God and other committed Christians in order to live out all that God has in store for us and to better discern what God wills and longs for us. Where some today may see holiness as unnatural and therefore not what we were created for, it is important to remember that what it means to be human is not bound up in what we are at present but more importantly what we are called to be and with whom we join in that calling.

Holiness amidst the Spiritual Disciplines

So what tools can we employ in order to better grasp this notion of holiness? Akin to the little prince's request, if the goal of our lives is to worship God and enjoy Him forever (as noted in the Westminster Catechism), we discover rather quickly that getting an accurate picture of God is a challenge. But like the aviator's box, the spiritual disciplines exist as a way of framing the search after God. The spiritual disciplines are practices that Christians throughout their history have assumed mark the Christian life. The phrase "spiritual discipline" is the bringing together of the spiritual and the bodily for the purpose of training and taming those parts of our nature that can distract us from God. They are also actions we engage in to remind us what is lovely and valued by the risen Lord. Spiritual disciplines train us toward the full life of faith. While everything can be used by God for the building up of faith, some things have been seen as more consistent and reliable for forming and taming us for the sake of the gospel.

John Wesley attended to these disciplines and talked about them in terms of the "means of grace." These can be divided into two broad categories, "works of piety" and "works of mercy," and within each category one can find both individual and collective practices.[9] Examples of these include the following:

- Works of Piety
  - Individual Practices
    - Prayer
    - Fasting
    - Searching the Scriptures
    - Healthy Living
  - Communal Practices
    - Holy Communion
    - Baptism
    - Christian Conferencing (gathering together in communities both large and small)
- Works of Mercy
  - Service focused toward individual needs
    - Doing Good (Good works)
    - Visiting the Sick
    - Visiting the Imprisoned
    - Feeding & Clothing Those in Need
    - Earning, Saving, & Giving All One Can
  - Service focused toward communal/societal needs
    - the Seeking of Justice; Opposition to Slavery

9. See Wesley's sermon "On Zeal" for a deeper discussion of these categories.

In addition to Wesley, others have elaborated on the spiritual disciplines in the Christian life. Two popular and thoughtful writers in recent years have been Dallas Willard and Richard Foster. Willard describes the importance of both disciplines of abstinence (inward) and disciplines of engagement (outward) whereas Foster speaks of inward, outward, and corporate disciplines. Take a look at the list that follows and review the ways each author notes activities that are both inward and external spiritual disciplines.

What are some that you are familiar with and which ones seem new?

Dallas Willard	Richard Foster
Disciplines of Abstinence	*Inward Disciplines*
Solitude	Meditation
Silence	Prayer
Fasting	Fasting
Frugality	Study
Chastity	
Secrecy	*Outward Disciplines*
Sacrifice	Simplicity
	Solitude
Disciplines of Engagement	Submission
Study	Service
Worship	
Celebration	*Corporate Disciplines*
Service	Confession
Prayer	Worship
Fellowship	Guidance
Confession	Celebration
Submission	

(Cited from Dallas Willard, *The Spirit of the Disciplines*, 158 and Richard Foster, *Celebration of Discipline*)

One of the common threads you will note in both lists is the role that the inward life plays in the spiritual disciplines. This emphasis on interiority is the contemplative life of reflection. Many writers in the Christian tradition have worked to define what contemplation means. Walter Burghardt understands contemplation to be "a long loving look at the real."[10] Ronald Rolheiser states to be contemplative "is to experience an event fully, in all its aspects. Biblically this is expressed as a knowing 'face to face.'"[11] Foster writes; "Put simply, the contemplative life is the steady gaze of the soul upon the God who loves us."[12] Elsewhere he declares, "Contemplative prayer is a loving attentiveness to God."[13] Finally, *The New Dictionary of Catholic Spirituality* maintains: "While contemplation has to do with the presence of God, it should not be thought of as making 'acts of the presence of God.' It is rather a way of making oneself aware of the presence of God who is always there."[14] The common thread that unites these various definitions is that contemplation is a loving and sustained gaze upon God and God's creation. It is far more about noticing and admiring God's presence than it is about becoming absorbed into the divine essence. In order to continue this steady gaze on the divine, spiritual disciplines help us continually to frame our gaze and walk in the paths of righteousness.

The Path of Holiness—Purgation, Illumination, and Union

So what does this path of holiness look like? For centuries, the call to holiness has been framed in a number of different ways

10. "Contemplation: A Long Loving Look at the Real," 15.

11. *The Shattered Lantern*, 20.

12. *Streams of Living Water*, 49.

13. *Prayer*, 158.

14. Shannon, "Contemplation, Contemplative Prayer," 209. This entry also provides a brief but helpful summary of the distinctions between the kataphatic and apophatic pathways to contemplative spirituality.

within Christianity. One way has been to see the movement of holiness as drawing close to the living God through being emptied, awakened, and united in deep and abiding relationship. In the mystical traditions of the church, this three-fold movement is seen as a call of continuous purgation, illumination and union.

Purgation: To Be Emptied so that We Hear Anew

For the mystics, the beginning of living a holy life is the movement of purgation or *purgatio*. In this stage people can be brought to awareness that they are not fully present to themselves or to the world around them and so something has to give. Think of this moment as a cold splash of water to the face, tripping on our own feet, or a song that breaks through all the emotional and spiritual static and white noise that clouds our hearts and minds and brings forth that resonant frequency of pure meaning. In the mystical tradition of Christianity, this moment is when someone struggles to gain control of "the flesh" and its disordered desires (like gluttony, lust, and the desire for possessions) in hopes of finding meaning and purpose beyond such things. This attempt to break the cycle of meaninglessness occurs sometimes as an active purging and emptying and at others as a passive event that is not planned.

Active purgation or intentional emptying is when the conscientious contemplative actively seeks release from that which clouds one's true identity, which is the *imago Dei* ("image of God"). This act is most often attributed to the practice of the spiritual disciplines. Through these practices, we become aware of things in our lives that need to be changed in order to hear God anew. This active purgation can take the form of times of silence, reading the Scriptures, fasting, working humbly at menial tasks, confessing, and seeking forgiveness to unburden and therefore release those things of the soul that bind the heart.

Passive purgation or unintentional emptying of the soul occurs when we are confronted with events or even people that are at once surprising, unexpected, and therefore beyond our control. These moments of passive purgation or unintentional emptying can feel like we have had our pocket picked—we do not notice what has happened until we reach for what we think is there only to find that it is now gone. This process can occur with revelations of wonder and amazement that bring us joy (like when we meet someone whom we instantly become smitten with), or it can be tragic when we are thrust into moments or events of suffering and crisis. Whether it be joy or suffering, during silence or the rhythmic beat of a snare drum, this movement of purgation or emptying of the soul occasions the release of that which we find so essential so that we can become open to the possibility of new ways of being and, more importantly, new or renewed relationships that will bring us there. Ignatius of Loyola, the founder of the Jesuit order, spells out the ways in which purgation is both active and passive:

> God who loves us creates us and wants to share life with us forever. Our love response takes shape in our praise and honor and service of the God of our life./All the things in this world are also created because of God's love and they become a context of gifts, presented to us so that we can know God more easily and make a return of love more readily./As a result, we show reverence for all the gifts of creation and collaborate with God in using them so that by being good stewards we develop as loving persons in our care for God's world and its development. But if we abuse any of these gifts of creation or, on the contrary, take them as the center of our lives, we break our relationship with God and hinder our growth as loving persons./In everyday life, then, we must hold ourselves in balance before all created gifts insofar as we have a choice and are not bound by some responsibility. We should not fix our desires on health or sickness, wealth or poverty, success or failure, a long life or a short one. For everything has the potential of calling forth in us a more loving response to our life forever with God./ Our only desire and our one choice should be this: I want

and I choose what better leads to God's deepening life in me.[15]

Illumination: When Hearing Becomes Seeing Anew

Through our engagement with the spiritual disciplines in which our hearts and minds are opened to being tamed in a holy way as we seek earnestly after the face of the living God, we come to find that the "same old, same old" of our life doesn't cut it any longer. It is at this point that the Christian mystical experience of illumination (*illuminatio*) takes place. During this period the contemplative learns the paths of holiness revealed in the gospel story and seeks to make sense of them in relation to other people. As we engage our lives more deeply through the practice of the spiritual disciplines and become open hearted to what God has in store, we see our lives and the lives of others not through the false light of our own brokenness but through the clear and piercing reality of the divine. This seeking after illumination is a search for something that is beyond us—a creative spark, an imagination that is aglow with possibilities, a drive to make something new in a world that is derivative. Also, much of this journey of illumination is the discovery of the transcendent which shapes the life of the everyday—things like love, caring, compassion, hope, faith, wonder, ecstasy, and awe—those things that can't be bottled or framed on the wall, yet when lived out, even for the briefest moment, they carry us out of ourselves and bind us to the hearts of others.

For the Carmelite mystic following in the ways of John of the Cross, the life and teachings of Christ, and in particular what Christ proclaimed and taught in the Sermon on the Mount (Matt 5–7), become more than merely a historical footnote but a syllabus by which to orient everything. The Christian monk lives a

15. St. Ignatius of Loyola as paraphrased by Fleming, *Draw Me into Your Friendship*, 27.

life of humility in the Spirit of God and by stretching the self to be formed and reformed in relationship to others who are seeking a similar vision. In this way, spiritual disciplines lead us not into boring practices that restrict us from living to the fullest but rather they open us to the illumination of all that life was meant to be in its height, depth and breadth. We are moved and trained in this taming of the spiritual disciplines to walk in the light fully.

Union: Experiencing the Embrace of God and Others

One of the most important things to remember about the importance of the spiritual disciplines in relation to holiness is that we were never called to live merely for ourselves and our own self-development. As we are tamed into holiness and framed by God's love by walking with God in both adoration and action, we are reminded of God's grace, and we recall it for and with those who are our neighbors. The illumination stage for the mystic takes one to the strangest place of all: the binding of one's life to the lives of others while seeking to live life not as an individual but as part of something that only makes sense when it is shared with others. For the Christian mystic, this final stage is union (*unitio*), a period when one's soul and the Spirit of God are bonded together in a union often described as the marriage depicted in the Song of Solomon (also called the Song of Songs or the Canticle of Canticles) because this union is so intimate and essential to what this new life is after purgation and illumination. This moment of ecstatic union is often marked by ineffable joy, exaltation, and proclamation, the latter of a kind that is at once also ineffable and moves us beyond language itself. Nevertheless, as liberating and vital as this moment of union with God and others is, we need to continue in the spiritual practices so that we will be sustained and prodded to probe deeper into the spiritual life.

Spiritual Disciplines and Humility

Finally, it is always important to remember that the spiritual disciplines are to be undertaken with a humble heart. A wonderful illustration of this humility is a sixth century desert monk who was seeking to study the scriptures:

> They tell the story of another old man who persevered in fasting for seventy weeks, eating only once a week. He asked of God about [the meaning of] a certain passage in holy Scripture and God did not reveal it to him. He said to himself, "See how much labour I have undertaken and it has been of no profit to me. I will go, therefore, to my brother and ask him about it." He went outside and closed the door to go out and an angel of the Lord was sent to him, saying, "The seventy weeks you fasted did not make you any closer to God. Now, because you have been humbled and are going off to your brother, I have been sent to explain the passage to you." He opened to him what he sought and then went away.[16]

As we can see in this story, marshalling all our willpower and might is not what brings us to holiness. Some will seek to manage God through a righteousness and morality that lack true heart and a willingness to listen and learn. As was discovered by the monk in this tale, it was only when he was willing to set aside his striving for perfection that the beginning of perfection could be attained. In short, when we let go of our striving and are released into humility, we begin along the path of holiness, one that is fitting for all Christians at all times and places.

16. As quoted in Casey, *Sacred Reading*, 44.

10

The Community of Holiness

David R. Nienhuis

WHAT ARE THE CHARACTERISTICS of a community of holiness? What are its distinctive practices and commitments? What does holiness look like "on the ground," in the real world of human relationships? A complete answer to these questions would of course extend far beyond the bounds of this short chapter, but one way forward is to draw a connection between our understanding of God's holiness and the church's ministry of reconciliation.

Trinitarian Holiness

As already alluded to in this collection, holiness is classically de-fined in terms of *separation*. To call God holy is to say that the Creator God is thoroughly different and purely "other" in relation to the created things of this world. A passage that illustrates this point is Isaiah 55:8–9, "For my thoughts are not your thoughts, nor are your ways my ways, says the Lord. For as the heavens are higher than the earth, so are my ways higher than your ways and my thoughts than your thoughts." But because God is love (1 John 4:8), God's holy otherness is oriented *toward us* and *for us*. Yes, God is always beyond us in the person of the Father, but

God is also with us in the person of the Son and within us and among us in the person of the Holy Spirit. With a trinitarian understanding, then, we see that God's holiness involves real *separation without withdrawal*, actual *difference without any distance*. God's holiness is an otherworldliness that is lovingly revealed in our world for us and for our salvation. Another passage from Isaiah makes the point: "For thus says the high and lofty one who inhabits eternity, whose name is Holy: I dwell in the high and holy place, and also with those who are contrite and humble in spirit, to revive the spirit of the humble, and to revive the heart of the contrite" (Isa 57:15).

When this loving, holy God works in our lives (both individually and communally), this pattern of being separated out from the world in order to love the world is replicated in us. When we commit to following the Lord with all our heart, soul, mind and strength, the Spirit of holiness immediately launches a process of differentiation in us that progressively detaches us from the practices, thought-systems, and communities that disciple us into worldliness. But again, this Spirit-driven, separating act does not end in our being hidden away in safe, sectarian seclusion from the world. Instead, it enables us to imitate God's Son Jesus, whose pure, holy adherence to the will of the Father empowered him to enter entirely into the reality of broken human existence, pouring himself out in self-emptying service as God's servant for the transformation of the world. This Spirit-empowered "pouring out" that enables us to give ourselves over to the will of the triune God for the healing of the world is the preeminent characteristic of Christian holiness.

The Ministry of Reconciliation

The Apostle Paul calls this loving act of divine self-giving *reconciliation*. Our English word comes from the Latin verb *reconciliare*, literally "to meet, agree, or unite again." A context of relational brokenness is assumed; people living in a fractured relationship come to meet or agree again and are thus considered reconciled. But the original language of the New Testament is Greek, and a look at the particular word used in that tongue reveals an even deeper, more overtly Christian nuance. The core of the Greek New Testament word-group that we translate "reconciliation" is a root that means "other" (-all). With an additional verb ending (-allassō), one has a construct that suggests "to make other," often rendered "to exchange." Finally, with the addition of an intensifying Greek prefix (kata-), the word becomes katallassō, "to make thoroughly other." When it is used in the context of human relationships, it might be rendered "to exchange thoroughly with another person."

In Paul's powerful articulation of Christian faith, this term functions as a shorthand expression for the transformative exchange the God of holiness accomplished for us in the person and work of Jesus Christ; as he puts it, "God proves his love for us in that while we still were sinners Christ died for us. . . . For if while we were enemies, we were reconciled to God through the death of his Son, much more surely, having been reconciled, will we be saved by his life" (Rom 5:8, 10).

Note the logic of exchange in this passage: We were standing as God's enemies, hostile to God's will and God's ways, but happily our holy God operates in a manner wholly different than humans who withdraw in anger or seek revenge. Instead, in an act of immeasurable mercy, God sent the Son into the world to exchange with us, to take our place, to live and die as one of us that he might destroy the power of death that fuels hostility and domination in our world. In his resurrection from the dead Jesus conquered that power along with the hate and fear it cultivates in us and among us. And now that the power of death has been permanently disabled, the resurrected Jesus calls us out of our "worldly ways" to follow his path of Spirit-empowered self-giving for the sake of others so that we, like him, might be resurrected to a new life of peace and love in God (for instance, see Rom 6:1–11 and Col 1:15–23).

To summarize: Holy people are those who are separated out by God and empowered by the Spirit to imitate Jesus, transforming hostility into peace through loving, self-giving exchange with others.

The Holiness of Reconciliation in Earliest Christianity

Earliest Christian communities understood that this logic of exchange rested at the core of their discipleship. They were called to imitate Jesus' self-giving in all their actions (though most especially in the way they treated their enemies) in order to function as a kind of signpost for all the world to see so that everyone might have a concrete illustration of the fact that God's reconciliation is real. "You are the light of the world," Jesus tells his disciples, so "let your light shine before others, so that they may see your good works and give glory to your Father in heaven" (Matt 5:14–16). Paul prefers more political language: "In Christ God was reconciling the world to himself, not counting their trespasses against them, and entrusting the message of reconciliation to us. So we are ambassadors for Christ, since God is making his appeal through us" (2 Cor 5:19–20). The church is called to be an embassy for the kingdom of God, representing that kingdom in a foreign and sometimes hostile territory.

How is the Christian community called to make God's holiness known to the world? Despite many contemporary Christian practices, Paul strongly asserts that a true community of the Holy Spirit is not characterized by its exciting worship, powerful preaching, or claims of pop-cultural "relevance." No, a truly Spirit-filled holy community is characterized by its supernatural ability to rise above the divisions and hostilities that characterize our world in order to live in it as a signpost of God's reign. Note, for instance, that Paul's articulation of the fruit of the Spirit describes the characteristics of a community capable of living and worshiping together in peace: "The fruit of the Spirit is love, joy, peace, patience, kindness, generosity, faithfulness, gentleness, and self-control" (Gal 5:22–23). Let's put it sharply: According to this list, the fruit of the Spirit are *community-forming* and *community-sustaining* virtues.

Now consider how Paul speaks to the Corinthian church, one that was caught up in communal in-fighting and conflict: "I could not speak to you as spiritual people, but rather as people of the flesh, as infants in Christ. . . . For as long as there is jealousy and quarreling among you, are you not of the flesh, and behaving according to human inclinations?" (1 Cor 3:1, 3). Again, let's put it sharply: *We know people are spiritual by their capacity to love the way Jesus loved.* As it says in the first letter of John, "Whoever says 'I abide in him,' ought to walk just as he walked. . . . Those who say, 'I love God,' and hate their brothers or sisters, are liars; for those who do not love a brother or sister whom they have seen, cannot love God whom they have not seen" (1 John 2:6; 4:20). This Christ-patterned life is what it means to be "holy" and "separate" from the world.

The Contemporary Challenge

This challenge isn't simply a matter of "getting along" with a community of like-minded people, ones we already know and like. Many church communities are often simply centers of sameness, social clubs where like-minded people gather together in order to reinforce what might be called "self-securing communal identities." A "self-securing communal identity" is one that maintains clear community boundaries—sometimes overtly, sometimes in hidden ways—in order to separate itself and to protect its members from the sort of people that have been labeled as "other." It has been shown, for instance, that ninety percent of American churches are made up of congregations that are at least ninety percent racially similar. American churches are likewise divided economically, with rich people and poor people typically worshiping separately.[1] And the list goes on and on: There are conservative churches and liberal churches, "traditional" churches with choirs and "contemporary" churches with pop-music worship bands, liturgical churches and "free" churches, churches that encourage personal piety and churches that emphasize social justice, churches that are pro-America and churches that are critical of America, churches that cater to middle-class families and others to hip, young singles. America is a kind of religious marketplace where consumers are invited to shop around in order to select the brand of Christian community that will do the best job of meeting their self-determined "needs."

But these churches do not reflect their call to be communities of trinitarian holiness, for as indicated by the way they secure their communal identity, they tend to overcome human hostility not by the power of the Holy Spirit but by the effort to keep "different" people at a distance. But in the face of this cheap, easy, worldly unity, Jesus says, "If you love those who love you, what reward do you have? Do not even the tax collectors do the same? And if you greet only your brothers and sisters, what more are you doing than others? Do not even the Gentiles do the same?" (Matt 5:46–47). It is easy to love as the world loves. If we are to love as our holy God loves, we must pursue a far more difficult way of joining together in community.

Indeed, the world is divided economically, but a holy community will commit to providing a space where rich and poor interact.[2] The world is divided by race, ethnicity and nationality, but a holy community will strive to cross these boundaries by embracing believers "from every nation, from all tribes and peoples and languages" (Rev 7:9). The world encourages us to rigidly over-determine gender roles, boxing people into culturally-shaped depictions of what it means to be a man or woman,

1. A startling account of these discrepancies can be found in Emerson and Smith, *Divided by Faith*, 16.

2. A number of passages illustrate this theme; see for instance Acts 4:32–35; 1 Cor 11:17–34; Jas 2:1–5, 14–17; and 1 John 3:17–18.

99

but in a holy community "there is no longer male and female, for all of you are one in Christ Jesus" (Gal 3:28). The world is often characterized by loud-mouthed and divisive punditry, partisanship, and slander, but in holy community believers commit to "do nothing from selfish ambition or conceit, but in humility [they] regard others as better than" themselves, looking "not to [their] own interests, but to the interests of others" (Phil 2:3–4). The world is characterized by enmity and strife, but a holy community will not allow such things to persist in its ranks. "Bless those who persecute you," Paul insists, "bless and do not curse them. Rejoice with those who rejoice, weep with those who weep. Live in harmony with one another; do not be haughty, but associate with the lowly; do not claim to be wiser than you are. Do not repay anyone evil for evil, but take thought for what is noble in the sight of all. If it is possible, so far as it depends on you, live peaceably with all" (Rom 12:14–18). Again, a trinitarian understanding of holiness involves real *separation* without *withdrawal*, actual *difference* without *distance*. The Spirit separates us from worldly practices of divisiveness so that we can be devoted to loving one another as God loves us.

Reconciliation in Christian Worship

There is no easy human formula for creating a community of holiness, for as Paul reminds us, reconciliation is ultimately a miracle that God accomplishes in us and among us (2 Cor 5:18). Nevertheless, Scripture provides us with such a rich vision of reconciliation that we are often able to identify and celebrate it when it is made manifest in our midst.

Within the worshiping practices of the church, reconciliation is most powerfully expressed in the liturgical celebrations of baptism and Eucharist (the latter is known variously as "Communion," "the Lord's Supper," or "the Mass"). These crucially important ancient practices were commanded by the Lord himself for good reason.[3] Baptism is the act of *communal initiation* wherein individual believers are separated out from the world to participate spiritually in the death and resurrection of Christ. Among other things, the going down into the water symbolizes the death of the self (see Rom 6:3 and Col 2:12), while the rising up out of the water symbolizes our resurrection to a new life of participation in Jesus' self-giving in service to others (see Rom 6:4, 1 Cor 12:12–13, and Col 2:12). Eucharist corresponds to baptism as the act of *communal nurture*; in and through it, believers remember Jesus' self-giving sacrifice in the past (1 Cor 11:26), celebrate the Spirit's work of drawing us into selfless unity in the present (1 Cor 10:16–17), and anticipate the goal of perfect communion with God and one another in the kingdom of heaven in the future (see Rev 19:19).

Combined, these two ancient acts proclaim the essential message of salvation we have been describing in this chapter: Through the work of Christ and the Spirit, our Holy God separates us out from the world to draw us into the ministry of reconciliation. God does this by turning selfish people into servants, egocentric individuals into loving members, and enemies into friends. Churches that honor these Christian rituals remind us as congregants that we do not participate in church principally to be fed, to have *our* needs met on *our* terms, to worship according to *our* preferred style and to hear sermons that align with *our* personal commitments. Instead, church participation is an enlistment into a Spirit-driven holiness movement designed to transform the world.

Reconciliation in the Work of Christian Organizations and Individuals

Though we rarely hear such things reported in the popular news media, evidence of God's reconciling work abounds in our world

3. For example, look at the following passages: Matt 26:26–29 and 28:18–20; Mark 14:22–25; Luke 22:14–20; and 1 Cor 11:23–25.

today. For instance, we notice such evidence in those individuals and organizations who are not content to live with the divisions that characterize the Christian church, knowing that our brokenness threatens the integrity of our witness to the world (see John 17:20–23). Dozens of Protestant and Catholic leaders have joined together to form a group called *Evangelicals and Catholics Together*, which has spent the last three decades looking very closely at what actually divided Protestants and Catholics in the past in order to see if those issues require us to be separated any longer.[4] Through their work we are facing the fact that a lot of what divides Christians has less to do with essential doctrines and more to do with mutual stereotyping, misunderstanding, and entrenched indifference.

Other Christian organizations enter directly into areas of world hostility to provide a distinctive witness to God's reconciliation. A good example is an organization in Jerusalem called Musalaha (the Arabic word for "reconciliation").[5] Musalaha promotes reconciliation between Israeli and Palestinian Christians so that they in turn might act as a witness to their larger respective communities. One of their key practices is known as the Desert Encounter, which takes mixed groups of Palestinians and Israelis on a journey through the wildernesses of the Sinai, Negev, and Jordan, requiring them to share camels and other resources along the way. Everyone must cross social and ideological boundaries to work together to negotiate the hardship of their mutual task. Along the way they learn to communicate, and as a result, cultural enemies are transformed into Christian friends.

We can also see the holiness of reconciliation at work in the selfless acts of Christian individuals who live out the call of Christ in the midst of difficult circumstances. One contemporary example is that of Ginn Fourie, a South African Christian woman whose daughter was gunned down by militants from

4. See the books edited by Charles Colson and Richard John Neuhaus: *Evangelicals and Catholics Together* and *Your Word is Truth*.

5. For more information, see the Musalaha website at www.musalaha.org.

the Pan-African Congress as the apartheid system was crumbling in the early 1990s. Ginn was not content simply to see her daughter's murderers be convicted and sent to prison for their crime. Instead, she publicly forgave her daughter's killers, and out of that forgiveness a series of relationships was forged that resulted in the creation of a foundation that has worked ever since to transform the socio-political reality of South Africa by teaching reconciliation and providing healing and job training for former combatants.[6]

Of course, the vast majority of God's holy reconciling work occurs "under the radar" in the many unspectacular ways everyday Christians open their hearts and bridge cross-cultural boundaries to embrace those around them. It happens when churches open their doors to sit down for meals together with the homeless people in their midst. It happens when Christians walk down the street to get to know a neighbor from another culture. It happens when we take the time to actually listen to those with whom we disagree. It happens whenever holy people and communities offer up to the world a tangible manifestation of the good news that God has already reconciled the world in Christ. It is in this regard that the Christian community is called to be holy, separating itself from the practices of this world to work in partnership with the God of holiness. Paul quintessentially puts the matter in the following way for the Corinthian church, and the charge still applies today:

> So if anyone is in Christ, there is a new creation: everything old has passed away; see, everything has become new! All this is from God, who reconciled us to himself through Christ and has given us the ministry of reconciliation; that is, in Christ God was reconciling the world to himself, not counting their trespasses against them, and entrusting the message of reconciliation to us. So we are ambassadors for Christ, since God is making his appeal through us; we entreat you on behalf of Christ, be

6. Ginn's story is more fully elaborated in De Gruchy, *Reconciliation*, 165–7.

reconciled to God. For our sake he made him to be sin
who knew no sin, so that in him we might become the
righteousness of God (2 Cor 5:17–21)

11

Holiness and Mission

Michael D. Langford

SOME MIGHT DISMISS ANY connection made between holiness
and mission as tenuous, perhaps even paradoxical. After all,
doesn't holiness refer to separation from the culture at large and
mission to engaging it? Doesn't holiness emerge from "religion
that is pure and undefiled before God" in which the Christian
must "*keep oneself unstained by the world*"?[1] And doesn't mission emerge from the final command of Jesus to "*Go into all the
world* and proclaim the good news to the whole creation"?[2] Don't
mission and holiness really form two ends of a dialectic that the
believer must hold in tension as one who is "in but not of the
world"?[3]

1. See James 1:27. I use italics here to contrast the seemingly alternate commands of keeping oneself from the world, as suggested here, and engaging
the world, as commanded in the Great Commission: "Go therefore and make
disciples of all nations, baptizing them in the name of the Father and of the
Son and of the Holy Spirit, and teaching them to obey everything that I have
commanded you" (Matt 28:19–20a).

2. See Mark 16:15.

3. This well-known theological dictum is taken from John 17:15–16, which
is part of Jesus' parting prayer for his disciples: "I am not asking you to take
them out of the world, but I ask you to protect them from the evil one. They do
not belong to the world, just as I do not belong to the world." It is interesting

As it has been stated in this book, a common conception of holiness is one in which the Christian is "set apart" from the sin endemic to the culture that surrounds her; furthermore, a common conception of mission is one in which the Christian who is "sent"[4] into that culture must strive to maintain her holiness as she follows Jesus' mandate to "be my witnesses in Jerusalem, in all Judea and Samaria, and to the ends of the earth."[5] These notions of holiness and mission are sometimes held apart as two magnetic poles, each with its own pull on the believer—one an imperative of righteousness and the other an imperative of responsibility. Perhaps this dialectic is merely the theological embodiment of the two "Tablets of the Law," the first commanding fidelity to God and the second to neighbor.[6] Perhaps holiness and mission reflect Jesus' own two-part summation of faithfulness when he declared that the two greatest commandments are to love God with all that we are and to love our neighbor as ourselves.[7] Per-

---

to note the next two verses: "Sanctify them in the truth; your word is truth. As you have sent me into the world, so I have sent them into the world." Jesus here seems to be making a connection between his own identity and that of his disciples as being "sent . . . into the world." Further on, we will see the significance of this identification for the theological connection between holiness and mission.

4. "Mission" means, literally, "being sent," "sent out," or "sendingness."

5. See Acts 1:8.

6. I refer here, of course, to the Ten Commandments, or "Decalogue," which is sometimes divided into two sections, the first four commandments describing righteousness in relation to God and the final six considering righteousness in relation to neighbor. However, according to Jesus' clarification or "radicalization" of the Law, this distinction may be much blurrier than it is often made out to be. Righteousness before God and righteousness before neighbor are interrelated.

7. See Matthew 22:36–40. Ironically, neither of these two commandments is part of the Decalogue and yet Jesus said that on "these two commandments hang all the law and the prophets." The first, "You shall love the Lord your God with all your heart, and with all your soul, and with all your mind," is a paraphrase of Deuteronomy 6:5, "You shall love the Lord your God with all your heart, and with all your soul, and with all your might." This is part of the *Shema*, which is central to the Torah and to Jewish worship. The second, "You shall love your neighbor as yourself," is a paraphrase of Leviticus 19:18,

haps these two commandments are a systematic and progressive form of discipleship whereby a believer first establishes her holiness and then proceeds to engage the culture around her (but carefully so in order to not compromise her holiness).

However, in light of theological and scriptural understandings of holiness and mission, we cannot so cleanly make a distinction between the two. In fact, as we will see, each is implicit in the other. In other words, to be holy is to engage in mission, and to engage in mission is to be holy. And, as we will also see, they are bound together in love.

Theological Holiness & Mission

The concept of "mission" is often understood strictly in terms of the particular missionary activities of the church, or as "missions." Some imagine mission to involve carrying the gospel message to non-Christians, usually in some distant land, so that they may come to "accept Jesus as Lord and savior." Understood this way, mission is a sort of global evangelism.[8] Alternately, some imagine mission to involve doing good deeds for those in need, again usually in foreign locales. Understood this way, mission is global relief or development work.[9]

"You shall not take vengeance or bear a grudge against any of your people, but you shall love your neighbor as yourself: I am the Lord." This passage is part of a section of Leviticus that actually discusses the nature of holiness, which illustrates the connection between love of neighbor and holistic righteousness that Jesus was making.

8. The word "evangelism," comes from the Greek word *euangelion*, which means "good news" or "gospel." However, is the *euangelion* spoken of in Scripture in fact only a cognitive assertion of Jesus as "Lord and savior"? Passages in books such as Isaiah, Matthew, Acts, and Romans seem to suggest that the good news is much broader than merely an assertion of belief.

9. By the middle of the twentieth century, the International Missionary Council (IMC) and the World Council of Churches (WCC)—the former was subsumed into the latter in 1962 to form the Committee on World Mission & Evangelism (CWME)—had largely come to understand "mission" in terms of relief work and not proclamation. However, is God's mission in Scripture

However, to understand mission strictly in either of these categories is to promote a reductionism.[10] Mission is not merely proclamation of the gospel so as to evince confession of faith, conversion, and church membership. Neither is mission merely relief work meant to ease physical or emotional burdens. Mission means, literally, "being sent." To engage in mission is nothing less than being sent out into the world, far and near, to engage the holistic work of God in which we have the privilege and responsibility of participating.

Rather than understanding mission in terms of "missions"—which locates it as activity of local congregations, parachurch organizations or personal endeavors—perhaps it is more appropriate to understand mission *theologically*, that is, within the logic of God's own being. God's very nature is related to mission. God is ontologically "ecstatic," meaning that God is, by nature, "reaching out"[11] to that which is not God, the latter including us. A trinitarian understanding of God images a God that is constantly being "sent" from God's own being to humanity. God the Father sent God the Son into the world (the Incarna-

truly only meant for the material needs of people? The activity of God in the persons of the Father, Son, and Holy Spirit seem to display work that is also proclamatory in nature.

10. This false dichotomy was exemplified by the conflict between the CWME on the one hand, and, on the other, the Lausanne Movement—born out of the Billy Graham Evangelistic Association—which largely emphasized "mission" in terms of proclamation and conversion. By the end of the 1970s, these two movements had become entrenched in their different understandings of mission. In reaction to the rapid growth of the Lausanne Movement, and in an attempt to recover the importance of proclamation and conversion in mission, the CWME published *Mission & Evangelism–An Ecumenical Affirmation* in 1982; the title itself illustrates that the two organizations considered relief work and proclamation, "mission" and "evangelism," to be distinct goals with one having priority over the other. This, of course, displays a reductionism in meaning for both terms.

11. The word "ecstatic" comes from the prefix *ek*, meaning "out from," and the root word *stasis*, meaning "state of equilibrium or rest." God is "ecstatic" in that God is constantly going out from God's own perfect being—not because God must, but because God freely chooses to be God in such a way.

tion) so that God and humanity might be reconciled. God the Father and God the Son sent God the Holy Spirit (Pentecost) so that the reconciliation between God and humanity might then be redeemed in the lives of God's people. This movement of God toward us might be termed the *missio Dei*, the mission of God, or, literally, the "sendingness" of God. Mission is primarily and foundationally God's activity as God moves toward us in order to effect holistic and redemptive communion. Mission is who God is. It is what God does.

What, then, is our role in mission? For us, mission is participating in God's mission—a mission that has been going on since the dawn of time, and it will continue to go on until the end of time. God's mission was begun with the creation of the world; pledged in the covenant with Abraham; enacted in God's relationship with Israel; reified through the words and deeds of the prophets; actualized in the life, death and resurrection of Jesus Christ; personalized in the ongoing work of the Holy Spirit; and proclaimed to be one day fully revealed in the second coming of Christ. Yet God does not instantiate this mission into the world unilaterally. Scripture tells us that God has constantly worked in and through God's people in order to bring about salvation. God has chosen time and again to use us to carry out the *missio Dei*. God uses the Body of Christ, the church, to carry God's very presence—a presence embodied in faith, hope and love—into the world. This mission involves proclamation of the gospel, caring for those in need, seeking justice for the marginalized, evoking new confessions of faith, praying fervently, worshiping passionately, speaking boldly, and loving radically. In a word, our mission is to be an authentic and holistic *witness* to that which God has done, is doing, and will do in Jesus Christ by the power of the Holy Spirit.

It is for this reason that we might describe mission not in terms of an activity of the church but rather in terms of who we are as disciples—or, more accurately, *whose* we are as disciples. As followers of Jesus Christ, empowered by the Holy Spirit, we are caught up in God's mission. Rather than defining mission as the "missions" of some organization or set of individuals, we are people who have a "missional" identity by virtue of the mission in which we participate. Therefore, in terms of activity, we might understand mission as primarily and foundationally an activity of God, and secondarily and derivatively an activity of God's people. Or alternately, in terms of identity, we might understand God as a missional God and ourselves as a people who are missional by virtue of the fact that we are in Christ.

How does our missional identity and activity relate to holiness? To answer that question, we must remember that holiness, like mission, is first of all descriptive of God. Literally, to be holy is to be "set apart." God, as the one who *ex nihilo* ("out of nothing") created everything, is not part of creation. Likewise, God, as the source of all that is good,[12] is not part of the corruption of creation, namely sin. Sin disallows creation from existing according to its created essence of goodness. But God is not so corrupted. God is holy. God is, by nature, set apart. And yet God as uncorrupted also comes to us in the midst of our corruption in order to save us. God, then, is by nature both holy and missional, both "set apart" and "sent."

Is this, then, the same dialectical tension with which we began? Do holiness and mission contrast with one another even within God's own being and action? No, they do not.

12. As Jesus says in Matthew 19:17, "There is only one who is good." Christians understand "goodness" only in terms of God, never the reverse. That is, we define "good" by looking at who God is and what God does. We do not define for ourselves what is good and then attribute that definition to God. That would be committing the error with which Ludwig Feuerbach famously—and accurately—critiqued Christian theology: "The consciousness of the infinite is nothing else than the consciousness of the infinity of the consciousness; or, in the consciousness of the infinite, the conscious subject has for his object the infinite of his own nature" (Feuerbach, *The Essence of Christianity*, 2–3). Essentially, Feuerbach is saying that we commit the error of defining God in our own image, which led him to categorize theology as a practice of anthropology. His critique was similar to many made in the eighteenth and nineteenth centuries, causing many Christian theologians to reconsider the epistemological grounds of Christian theology.

Theologically, holiness and mission do not form a dialectical tension but rather a unity-in-distinction. Embedded within God's missional nature is also God's holiness. How so?

As mentioned, God is by nature part of neither creation nor sin. There is between God and creation an ontological divide, an "infinite qualitative difference."[13] However, in freedom, God wills to engage with creation for purposes of reconciliation and redemption, to overcome the corruption of sin. Because this movement of God toward, in, and for creation is an act committed in freedom, without necessity or compulsion, we might also understand this movement as God's grace (unmerited favor) and mercy (unwarranted remittance). This free and salvific movement is summed up under the description of God as "love." In love, God chooses to cross the ontological divide in order to engage with creation and save it from its own corruption. God is set apart from the corruption of sin and free to act according to God's own good nature. In freedom and love, God moves toward us to save us. In other words, it is precisely because of God's holiness, precisely because God is "set apart" from the corruption of sin, that God is free to love, free to move toward creation to reconcile with it and redeem it from its corruption.

In the being of God we find both holiness and mission. And God is both holy and missional not as a result of some dialectical tension; rather, God is missional as God is holy; holiness and mission are two distinct ways of understanding God within the unity of God's love. In love, God's mission is found in the midst of God's holiness.

We see these qualities of holiness and mission in the primary expressions of God's love, namely, the Incarnation and

---

13. This notion was one of the theological emphases of Søren Kierkegaard. "God and man are two qualities between which there is an infinite qualitative difference. Every doctrine which overlooks this difference is, humanly speaking, crazy; understood in a godly sense, it is blasphemy" (Kierkegaard, *Sickness Unto Death*, 106). This notion helped some theologians, in response to the critique of Feuerbach and others, to understand theology as reliable only if it is grounded in revelation, that is, God's words to us and not the reverse.

Pentecost. As the second and third persons of the Trinity, the Son and the Spirit are by nature different than the world, eternally "set apart" from it.[14] Church Fathers, following the biblical descriptions of the Son and the Spirit as "sent" into the world, termed the economic (or salvific) role of the second and third persons of the Trinity as the "divine missions" of God.[15] There is a unity-in-distinction between these two notions of the persons of God, first as they exist within God and second as they salvifically engage with the world.[16] The biblical names given to the second and third persons in their appropriated[17] interaction with creation—"Jesus Christ" and "Holy Spirit"—are telling. "Jesus" (meaning "God saves") reflects God's missional activity as God engages with the world in the Incarnation in order to reconcile divinity and humanity, and "Christ" (meaning "Anointed One")

14. This description of God's threefold form as it exists *in se* (in God's own being), apart from the world, is called the "immanent Trinity." A sustained—and still substantially authoritative—theological examination of the doctrine of the Trinity, in which these inner relationships of the Father, Son, and Spirit are described, is Augustine's *De Trinitate*, written in the early part of the fifth century.

15. See, for instance, Books II–IV of *De Trinitate*. The description of the threefold work of God as it exists *ad extra* (outside of God's being), in engagement with the world, is called the "economic Trinity."

16. Roman Catholic theologian Karl Rahner famously pointed out this identification in his theological dictum: "The 'economic Trinity' is the 'immanent Trinity' and the 'immanent Trinity' is the 'economic Trinity'" (Rahner, *The Trinity*, 22). Rahner was saying that because God's acts are authentic to God's being, to look at God's threefold interaction with creation is to perceive the threefold nature of God's being. The revelation of God is reliable, claimed Rahner. But, for our purposes here, we might also say that because the acts of God are authentic to God's being, the missions of God also include God's holiness. God missionally engages the world *as* a holy God, not in addition to being holy, subsequent to being holy, or as a prelude to holiness. God's missional nature is also God's holy nature.

17. The doctrine of appropriation states that though the entire Trinity is active in every work of God, different works are "appropriated" to different persons of the Trinity. For instance, though creation is attributed to the work of God the Father (or God the Creator), the whole Trinity—including God the Son and God the Spirit—are involved. Similarly, all of God is present in the works of God the Son and God the Spirit.

reflects one who is set apart for special and divine purposes. Likewise, "Holy Spirit" reflects God's missional activity as the Holy One who engages with the world at Pentecost in order to redeem humanity to its created and reconciled existence; "Spirit"—*ruach* in Hebrew and *pneuma* in Greek—implies vivification, the giving of life. Both Jesus Christ and the Holy Spirit image a loving God who, though holy, does not remain distant, but rather engages the world in order to save it from its own corruption.

In sum, the theological notions of mission and holiness are held together within the being and action of God, being and action that might also be understood in terms of love. Because God is a holy God, set apart from creation and its corruption, God is also a missional God who engages with creation in order to save it. When we embrace our missional identity as disciples, we participate in God's mission, and in so doing, we also participate in God's holiness. Just as our secondary and derivative mission is based on the primary and foundational mission of God, so also is our holiness based on the extent to which we are grounded in the love of God found in Christ by the power of the Holy Spirit. And, as such, our holiness will also result in the embrace of our missional identity as mediators of God's salvific movement in the world.

Biblical Holiness and Mission

We will not pursue here a comprehensive account of the biblical concept of holiness as it is covered well elsewhere in this work. But we will investigate some important concepts of holiness alluded to in Scripture in order to relate it to the notion of mission. In so doing we will see that just as mission is grounded in holiness, holiness is likewise grounded in mission.

Scripture seems to portray holiness in two distinct yet related manners. First of all, God is holy. We have already discussed the notion of holiness belonging primarily and foundationally to God, but it bears noting the extensive biblical witness to this notion. God is understood as distinct from the world, far above it, and therefore worthy of reverence. Old Testament prophets, especially Isaiah, refer to God as the "Holy One of Israel."[18] God was to be respected, worshiped, adored, and even feared as one without peer or rival. Indeed, God's self-proclaimed name given to Moses—YHWH, roughly translated, "I am who I am"[19]— seems to reflect the singularity of God, wholly other and beyond anything known.

Secondly, people are holy if and when God sets them apart for divine purposes. In the Old Testament, God admonishes those who are meant to be God's people to "be holy, for I am holy." There is a direct connection between God's holiness and the command for God's people to be concomitantly, perhaps consequently, holy.[20] Israel was to be different from the other nations who worshiped other gods. This difference was expressed in many ways—morally, socially, ritualistically, and politically.[21] As the people who worshiped the God of Abraham, Isaac, and Jacob, Israel was to live according to the Law given to them by God, a Law that both described the identity bestowed upon them and also enabled them to embrace their holiness. Thus a person—or sometimes a place or thing or name—was deemed "holy" to the extent that they were set aside for God's purposes, fulfilled the scriptural mandates for holiness, or adhered to the Law.[22]

While both manners of holiness—God's and ours—are spoken of in the Old Testament, a majority of the references to

---

18. Some commentators make the claim that the "Holy One of Israel" spoken of in Isaiah refers to the Messiah. However, at least several of the references to the Holy One of Israel seem to indicate God, that is, YHWH. See, for instance, Isaiah 1:4; 5:24; 10:20; 17:7; 30:15; 41:16; 41:20; 43:3; 45:11; 47:4; 54:5; 55:5. See also Psalms 71:22 and 89:18 and Jeremiah 50:29 and 51:5.

19. See Exodus 3:14.

20. See, for instance Leviticus 11:44, 45; 19:2; 20:7, 26; and 21:8.

21. See the so-called "Holiness Code" of Leviticus 17–26.

22. These are matters considered extensively in the chapter within this collection by Kelsie Gayle Job and Frank Anthony Spina.

holiness in the New Testament is to the second manner.[23] However, the connection between the two manners is maintained: "Be holy as I am holy."[24] Just as the Israelites were called to image God's holiness in order to differentiate themselves from other nations and other gods, so the burgeoning community of Christ-followers is called to do the same. Yet there is another dimension to this renewed call to holiness. Christ-followers are to embrace holiness also for purposes of differentiating their transformed lives from the lives that they lived before their encounter with Christ. As this book has repeatedly emphasized, this transformed and holy life is to be a witness to the presence and power of the continuing presence of the Holy Spirit.

What is the content of this transformed life? Jesus himself summed it up: "'You shall love the Lord your God with all your heart, and with all your soul, and with all your mind.' This is the greatest and first commandment. And a second is like it: 'You shall love your neighbor as yourself.' On these two commandments hang all the law and the prophets."[25] Jesus recalls the Jewish people to the original intent of the Law, namely, to orient them to the love of God and neighbor. That is what it meant—what it had always meant—to be God's holy people. Radical love set apart the children of God as different from those who are—or were—"children" of something else.[26] As people of a holy and

23. This theme is pointed out in Robert Wall's contribution to this volume.

24. In reference to the Leviticus dictum spoken of above, 1 Peter 1:15–16 says, "Instead, as he who called you is holy, be holy yourselves in all your conduct; for it is written, 'You shall be holy, for I am holy.'" Robert Drovdahl drew out this point nicely in his chapter.

25. Matthew 22:37–40.

26. In the New Testament, the people of God as defined by the person and work of Jesus are called "children of God," or "children of your Father in Heaven" (Matt 5:45); "children of the kingdom" (Matt 13:38); "children of the Most High" (Luke 6:35); "children of light" (Luke 16:8; John 12:36; Eph 5:8; 1 Thess 5:5); and "children of the promise" (Rom 9:8; Gal 4:28). Alternately, those who are not people of God as defined by the person and work of Jesus are called "children of the evil one" (Matt 13:38), "children of this age" (Luke 16:8), "children of the flesh" (Rom 9:8), "children of wrath" (Eph 2:3), and "children of the

loving God, Israel was to be a holy and loving people. The person and work of Jesus and the presence of the Holy Spirit not only drew people back to this truth but also transformed them, empowering them for a holy life of love that would witness to the holy God of love.

What has this to do with the mission of God's people? It is simply this: Jesus commissioned his disciples to carry on his message and work, a message and work of God's love, and that message and work are expressed in the holiness of those called by Jesus and transformed by the Holy Spirit. Disciples of Jesus were meant to be set apart from the world precisely by means of their mission in the world. Just as, theologically speaking, God's mission is embedded in God's holiness, so is, scripturally speaking, the holiness of God's people embedded in the mission of God's people.

In the Incarnation, God recalled us to the way of living for which we were created, namely, love of God and neighbor. At Pentecost, God empowered us to embrace that way of living. In both, God mediated the divine mission of love into the world by imparting to us the same mission. We as the people of God, the Body of Christ, and the community of the Holy Spirit have been created, commissioned, and empowered to be the bearers of God's love in word and deed. The mission of God, the reconciliation and redemption of God's corrupted creation, is carried out

---

devil" (1 John 3:10). The difference between these two groups of people is not cultic or national (as was often the case in the Old Testament) but rather revealed by the presence of the Holy Spirit, thereby enabling them to participate in God's love. Take as examples Ephesians 2:3–5 ("All of us once lived among them in the passions of our flesh, following the desires of flesh and senses, and we were by nature children of wrath, like everyone else. But God, who is rich in mercy, out of the great love with which he loved us even when we were dead through our trespasses, made us alive together with Christ"), Ephesians 5:8–9 ("For once you were darkness, but now in the Lord you are light. Live as children of light—for the fruit of the light is found in all that is good and right and true"), and 1 John 3:10 ("The children of God and the children of the devil are revealed in this way: all who do not do what is right are not from God, nor are those who do not love their brothers and sisters").

through us, and it is carried out in us precisely as we embrace our holiness. As followers of Jesus sent into the world to be his people, we are called to be holy, set apart for God's purposes as witnesses to God's love.

In sum, Scripture depicts the people of God as holy in light of God's holiness. This holiness is summed up in love; the people of God are set apart from the world by imaging God's holiness in their radical love of God and neighbor. Jesus commissions his disciples to this sort of holiness, sending his followers into the world with the transforming power of the Holy Spirit to mediate God's love through their witness. As his disciples, we too carry out the same mission, namely to witness to the transformative and holy love of God by means of our own love of God and neighbor, a love that ought to set us apart from the world. We embrace our mission by embracing our holiness. Our holiness is grounded in our missional identity. We live out our mission as Jesus' disciples by living as the holy people of God, people of radical love.

Conclusion

So, we see that holiness and mission are not two parts of a dialectical tension within the being and action of God, nor do they describe two separable or progressive parts in a life of discipleship. Rather, both holiness and mission are implied in each other, and they find their unity in love. To the extent that we are set apart from the world as people of God, we image and mediate God's love by engaging the world with that love. And to the extent that we are sent into the world as witnesses to the love of God, we live out our calling to be holy people who radically love God and neighbor. It is the love of God—mediated to us in the person and work of Jesus Christ and the transforming power of the Holy Spirit—that binds together our holiness and mission, and precisely as we carry that love into the world, it also finds its unity in us: "God's love was revealed among us in this way: God sent his only Son into the world so that we might live through him. In this is love, not that we loved God but that he loved us and sent his Son to be the atoning sacrifice for our sins. Beloved, since God loved us so much, we also ought to love one another. No one has ever seen God; if we love one another, God lives in us, and his love is perfected in us."[27]

27. 1 John 4:9–12.

Bibliography

Balthasar, Hans Urs von. *The Glory of the Lord.* Vol. 7. Edited by John Riches. Translated by Brian McNeil, CRV. San Francisco: Ignatius, 1989.

Bendroth, Margaret Lamberts. *Fundamentalism and Gender, 1875 to the Present.* New Haven, CT: Yale University Press, 1993.

Budde, Michael L., and John Wright, editors. *Conflicting Allegiances.* Grand Rapid: Brazos, 2004.

Burghardt, Walter J. "Contemplation: A Long Loving Look at the Real." *Church* (Winter 1989) 15–18.

Cagle, Mary Lee. *Life and Work of Mary Lee Cagle: An Autobiography.* Kansas City: Nazarene Publishing House, 1928.

Casey, Michael. *Sacred Reading: The Ancient Art of Lectio Divina.* Liguori, MO: Triumph, 1996.

Chia, Roland. "Salvation as Justification and Deification." *Scottish Journal of Theology* 64 (2011) 125–39.

Clark, Stephen B. *Man and Woman in Christ: An Examination of the roles of Men and Women in Light of Scripture and the Social Sciences.* Ann Arbor, MI: Servant, 1980.

Colson, Charles, and Richard John Neuhaus, editors. *Evangelicals and Catholics Together: Toward a Common Mission.* Dallas: Word, 1995.

———. *Your Word is Truth: A Project of Evangelicals and Catholics Together.* Grand Rapids: Eerdmans, 2002.

"Danvers Statement." In *Recovering Biblical Manhood and Womanhood*, edited by John Piper and Wayne Grudem, 469–72. Wheaton: Crossway, 1991.

Dawn, Marva J. *Reaching Out without Dumbing Down: A Theology of Worship for This Urgent Time.* Grand Rapids: Eerdmans, 1995.

De Gruchy, John W. *Reconciliation: Restoring Justice.* Minneapolis: Fortress, 2002.

Emerson, Michael O., and Christian Smith. *Divided by Faith: Evangelical Religion and the Problem of Race in America.* Oxford: Oxford University Press, 2000.

Feuerbach, Ludwig. *The Essence of Christianity.* Translated by Marian Evans. London: John Chapman, 1854.

Bibliography

Flannery, Christopher, and Rae Wineland Newstad. "The Classical Liberal Arts Tradition." In *The Liberal Arts in Higher Education: Challenging Assumptions, Exploring Possibilities*, edited by Diana Glyer and David L. Weeks, 3–23. Lanham, MD: University Press of America, 1998.

Fleming, David L., SJ. *Draw Me into Your Friendship: A Literal Translation and Contemporary Reading of the Spiritual Exercises*. Study Aids on Jesuit Topics 17. Saint Louis: Institute of Jesuit Sources, 1996.

Foster, Richard J. *Celebration of Discipline: The Path to Spiritual Growth*. 3rd ed. San Francisco: Harper: San Francisco, 1998.

———. *Prayer: Finding the Heart's True Home*. San Francisco: Harper San Francisco, 1992.

———. *Streams of Living Water: Celebrating the Great Traditions of Christian Faith*. San Francisco: Harper San Francisco, 1998.

Freitas, Donna. *Sex and the Soul: Juggling Sexuality, Spirituality, Romance, and Religion on America's College Campuses*. New York: Oxford, 2008.

Green, Joel B., and Mark D. Baker. *Recovering the Scandal of the Cross: Atonement in New Testament and Contemporary Contexts*. Downers Grove, IL: InterVarsity, 2000.

Hamm, Thomas D., editor. *Quaker Writings: An Anthology 1650–1920*. New York: Penguin, 2010.

Hauerwas, Stanley. *The State of the University: Academic Knowledges and the Knowledge of God*. Malden, MA: Blackwell, 2007.

Heclo, Hugh. *On Thinking Institutionally*. Boulder, CO: Paradigm, 2008.

Heitzenrater, Richard P. *Wesley and the People Called Methodists*. Nashville: Abingdon, 1995.

Ingersoll, Julie. *Evangelical Christian Women: War Stories in the Gender Battle*. New York: New York University, 2003.

Johnson, Elizabeth A. *She Who Is: The Mystery of God in Feminist Theological Discourse*. New York: Crossroad, 2001.

Kierkegaard, Søren. *Sickness Unto Death*. Radford, VA: Wilder, 2008.

Köstenberger, Andreas J. *God, Marriage, and Family: Rebuilding the Biblical Foundation*. Second edition. Wheaton: Crossway, 2010.

Kraybill, Donald B., Steven M. Nolt, and David L. Weaver-Zercher. *Amish Grace: How Forgiveness Transcended Tragedy*. San Francisco: Jossey-Bass, 2010.

Long, D. Stephen. *John Wesley's Moral Theology: The Quest for God and Goodness*. Nashville: Kingswood, 2005.

Mannermaa, Tuomo. "Justification and *Theosis* in Lutheran-Orthodox Perspective." In *Union with Christ: The New Finnish Interpretation of Paul*, edited by Carl E. Braaten and Robert W. Jenson, 25–41. Grand Rapids: Eerdmans, 1998.

Markham, Ian S. "The Idea of a Christian University." In *The Idea of a Christian University: Essays in Theology and Higher Education*, edited by Jeff Astley, Leslie Francis, John Sullivan, and Andrew Walker, 3–13. Milton Keynes, UK: Paternoster, 2004.

Marshall, Bruce D. "Justification as Declaration and Deification." *International Journal of Systematic Theology* 4 (2002) 3–28.

McClendon, James Wm., Jr., and James M. Smith. *Convictions: Defusing Religious Relativism.* Revised edition. Valley Forge: Trinity Press, 1994. Reprinted by Wipf & Stock, 2002.

Palmer, Phoebe. *Promise of the Father.* Boston: Henry V. Degen, 1859.

Peterson, Eugene H. *Subversive Spirituality.* Edited by Jim Lyster, John Sharon, Peter Santucci. Grand Rapids, MI: Eerdmans, 1997.

Peura, Simo. "What God Gives Man Receives: Luther on Salvation." In *Union with Christ: The New Finnish Interpretation of Paul,* edited by Carl E. Braaten and Robert W. Jenson, 76–95. Grand Rapids: Eerdmans, 1998.

Placher, William C. *The Domestication of Transcendence: How Modern Thinking about God Went Wrong.* Louisville: Westminster John Knox, 1996.

Rahner, Karl. *The Trinity.* Translated by Joseph Donceel. New York: Herder & Herder, 1970.

Raymond, Jonathan S. "Social Holiness: Journey, Exposures, Encounters." In *The Holiness Manifesto,* edited by Kevin W. Mannoia and Don Thorsen, 166–87. Grand Rapids: Eerdmans, 2008.

Roberts, B. T. *The Right of Women to Preach the Gospel.* Rochester: B. T. Roberts, n.d.

Rolheiser, Ronald. *The Shattered Lantern: Rediscovering a Felt Presence of God.* New York: Crossroad, 1995.

Saint-Exupéry, Antoine de. *The Little Prince.* New York: Harcourt Brace Jovanovich, 1943.

Sapiro, Virginia. *Women in American Society: An Introduction to Women's Studies.* Second edition. Mountain View, CA: Mayfield, 1990.

Scriven, Charles. "Schooling for the Tournament of Narratives." In *Theology without Foundations: Religious Practice and the Future of Theological Truth,* edited by Stanley Hauerwas, Nancey Murphy, and Mark Nation, 273–88. Nashville: Abingdon, 1994.

Shannon, William H. "Contemplation, Contemplative Prayer." In *The New Dictionary of Catholic Spirituality,* edited by Michael Downey, 209–14. Collegeville, MN: Liturgical, 1993.

Smith, James K. A. *Desiring the Kingdom: Worship, Worldview, and Cultural Formation.* Grand Rapids: Baker Academic, 2009.

Tangenberg, Katy. "Women's Mentoring on Christian Campuses: Balancing Tensions of Faith, Feminism, and Femininity." Paper presented to the Lilly Fellows Seminar on Gender and Christianity, Seattle Pacific University, 2010.

Vennard, Iva Durham. "Friendship with Christ" *Heart and Life* 18 (February 1929) 3.

Webster, John. *Holiness.* Grand Rapids: Eerdmans, 2003.

Wells, Samuel. *Improvisation: The Drama of Christian Ethics.* Grand Rapids: Eerdmans, 2004.

Bibliography

Wesley, John. "The Almost Christian." In *The Bicentennial Edition of the Works of John Wesley,* edited by Albert C. Outler, 1:131–41. Nashville: Abingdon, 1984.

———. "Hymn 490." In *The Bicentennial Edition of the Works of John Wesley,* edited by Franz Hildebrandt and Oliver A. Beckerlegge, 7:677–78. Nashville: Abingdon, 1983.

———. "The Lord Our Righteousness." In *The Bicentennial Edition of the Works of John Wesley,* edited by Albert C. Outler, 1:444–65. Nashville: Abingdon, 1984.

———. "The Nature, Design, and General Rules of the United Societies." In *The Bicentennial Edition of the Works of John Wesley,* edited by Rupert E. Davies, 9:69–73. Nashville: Abingdon, 1989.

———. "The Nature of Enthusiasm." In *The Bicentennial Edition of the Works of John Wesley,* edited by Albert C. Outler, 2:44–60. Nashville: Abingdon, 1985.

———. "The Scripture Way of Salvation." In *The Bicentennial Edition of the Works of John Wesley,* edited by Albert C. Outler, 2:152–69. Nashville: Abingdon, 1985.

———. "Upon Our Lord's Sermon on the Mount, Discourse 4." In *The Bicentennial Edition of the Works of John Wesley,* edited by Albert C. Outler, 1:531–49. Nashville: Abingdon, 1984.

———. "On Zeal." In *The Bicentennial Edition of the Works of John Wesley,* edited by Albert C. Outler, 3:308–21. Nashville: Abingdon, 1986.

Willard, Dallas. *The Spirit of the Disciplines: Understanding How God Changes Lives.* San Francisco: Harper and Row, 1988.

Wright, N. T. *Simply Christian: Why Christianity Makes Sense.* San Francisco: HarperSanFrancisco, 2006.